Sunshine Meadows

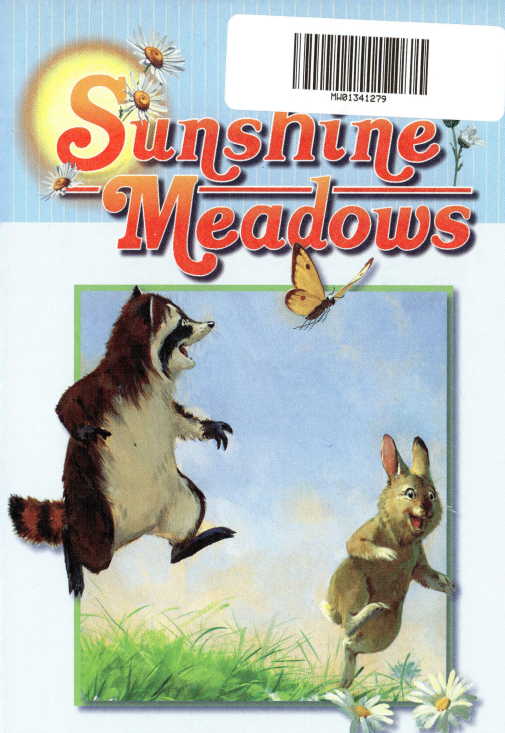

A Beka Book® Reading Program

Introduction

Children are eagerly searching for a workable sense of values. They need to see in the lives of great people, common people, and children like themselves, the unchanging values of the ages lived out. They need reading material that will give them ideals to reach for and examples to follow.

The stories in this reader have been selected from the readers of America's past and have been edited and modernized for student appeal and readability. This reader will introduce to children not only what is excellent in itself, but what their parents and grandparents have read before them—stories so good that they will never become old and stories that impart moral values.

These values are taught throughout the book—honesty, integrity, courage, faith, kindness, forgiveness, industry, unselfishness, patriotism, and respect for authority.

Thought questions at the end of the stories greatly aid in the understanding and appreciation of the selections.

Editors *Deborah Beck, Shela Conrad, Naomi Sleeth*

Art *Brian Jekel, Craig Granger, Frank Hicks, Jim Hutchinson*

Design *Michelle Johnson, Dawn Rash*

Copyright © 1996 Pensacola Christian College
All rights reserved. Printed in U.S.A. 2002 C00

No part of this publication may be reproduced or transmitted in any form or by any means, electronic or mechanical, including photocopy, recording, or any information storage and retrieval system, or by license from any collective or licensing body, without permission in writing from the publisher.

A Beka Book, a Christian textbook ministry of Pensacola Christian College, is designed to meet the need for Christian textbooks and teaching aids. The purpose of this publishing ministry is to help Christian schools reach children and young people for the Lord and train them in the Christian way of life.

"A Close Call" adapted from Molly Weiss, *Playmates, Book 2,* copyright © 1930 by D. C. Heath and Company. Reprinted by permission of Houghton Mifflin Company. *Angus and the Ducks* reprinted by permission of Harold Ober Associates Incorporated. Copyright 1930 by Doubleday & Co. "Thanksgiving" by Elizabeth Coatsworth reprinted by permission of her daughter Catherine B. Barnes.

Every reasonable effort has been made to trace owners of copyrighted materials in this book, but in some instances this has proven impossible. The publisher will be glad to receive information leading to more complete acknowledgments in subsequent printings of the book, and in the meantime extends apologies for any omissions.

Contents

Muddy Mouse *Helen and Alf Evers* 1
Why Drew Was Late *Author Unknown* 5
At Work and Play *Author Unknown* 8
The Puppy's Day *Author Unknown* 10
Looking for the Flag *Author Unknown* 14
Our Flag *Albert F. Blaisdell, Francis K. Ball* 18
Flags *Annette Wynne* 23
The Sea Horse *Author Unknown* 24
Rusty's Adventure *Seymour Reit* 27
Birds' Nests *Author Unknown* 34
Greta's Cow *Author Unknown* 39
The Boy and the Wind *Marie Zetterberg* 47
Don't Give Up the Ship *Edward Eggleston* 49
The Four Musicians *Adapted from Grimm* 54
A Cow in the House *Mabel Watts* 60
The Two Buckets *Adapted* 67
The Rain *Author Unknown* 68
The Army of Two *Mara L. Pratt* 70
United We Are Strong *An Aesop Fable* 75
The Good Shepherd
    Carolyn S. Bailey, Clara M. Lewis 77

The Lily *W. T. Vlymen* 83
A Close Call *Mollie Weiss* 84
What They Found *Carolyn Sherwin Bailey* 90
A Child's Garden of Verses *Author Unknown* 94
Singing *Robert Louis Stevenson* 97
The Swing *Robert Louis Stevenson* 98
Time to Rise *Robert Louis Stevenson* 99
Whole Duty of Children
   Robert Louis Stevenson 99
The Cow *Robert Louis Stevenson* 100
Rain *Robert Louis Stevenson* 101
Happy Thought *Robert Louis Stevenson* 101
The Miser *Retold from La Fontaine* 102
Helping Hands *Author Unknown* 105
A Cowboy's Day *Clyde Robert Bulla* 108
The Robins *Author Unknown* 113
The Story of Barry *Amelia McLester* 114
The Pilgrims *Author Unknown* 116
Thanksgiving *Elizabeth Coatsworth* 120
A Very Special Friend 122
Terri and the Gooseberries *Elizabeth Phelps* ... 130
Rabbits *Nancy Byrd Turner* 138
Topknot *A Swedish Folktale* 139
Dapple Grey's Friends
   Mary Laurence Turnbull Tufts 142
Old Mrs. Cricket *Author Unknown* 147
Lee and Traveller *Amelia McLester* 149
A Butterfly's Story *Mabel G. Folsom* 152
Why Does the Breeze Blow?
   Author Unknown 155

Fifteen Bathtubs *Margaret Wise Brown* 156
Lessons from Washington *Author Unknown* 161
Washington's Birthday *Author Unknown* 163
Thomas Edison *Amelia McLester* 164
The Bird's Lesson *George Macdonald* 170
Dare to Do Right *Albert N. Raub* 172
Speak the Truth *Author Unknown* 177
The Eagle and the Mole *Adapted from Krilof* 178
How Kong Fu Got His Name *Amelia McLester* 181
Ruth in the Harvest Field *Ella M. Powers,*
    Tho. M. Balliet 187
The Camel *Albert M. Raub* 192
The Seasons *Author Unknown* 197
The First Balloon *Author Unknown* 200
Angus and the Ducks *Marjorie Flack* 203
Frederick and His Page *Author Unknown* 208
The Owl *L. Alma-Tadema* 211

Sunshine Meadows
Guide to Character-Building Story Themes

Contentment
A Cow in the House, p. 60
Happy Thought, p. 101
The Two Buckets, p. 67
Topknot, p. 139
What They Found, p. 90

Courage
A Close Call, p. 84
Dare to Do Right, p. 172
How Kong Fu Got His Name, p. 181
The Army of Two, p. 70
The Good Shepherd, p. 77
The Pilgrims, p. 116
The Story of Barry, p. 114

Creation
A Butterfly's Story, p. 152
Birds' Nests, p. 34
Old Mrs. Cricket, p. 147
Rabbits, p. 138
The Camel, p. 192
The Good Shepherd, p. 77
The Lily, p. 83
The Sea Horse, p. 24
The Seasons, p. 197
Why Does the Breeze Blow? p. 155

Faith/Prayer
Thanksgiving, p. 120
The Pilgrims, p. 116

Family
Don't Give up the Ship, p. 49
Frederick and His Page, p. 208
Greta's Cow, p. 39
Ruth in the Harvest Field, p. 187
Terri and the Gooseberries, p. 130
The First Balloon, p. 200
United We Are Strong, p. 75

Forgiveness
A Very Special Friend, p. 122
Dare to Do Right, p. 172
Terri and the Gooseberries, p. 130

Friendship
A Close Call, p. 84
A Very Special Friend, p. 122
How Kong Fu Got His Name, p. 181
The Four Musicians, p. 54
The Pilgrims, p. 116

Gratitude
A Close Call, p. 84
Frederick and His Page, p. 208
How Kong Fu Got His Name, p. 181
Thanksgiving, p. 120
The Pilgrims, p. 116

Helpfulness/Service
Dapple Grey's Friends, p. 142
Frederick and His Page, p. 208
Helping Hands, p. 105
How Kong Fu Got His Name, p. 181
Ruth in the Harvest Field, p. 187
The Story of Barry, p. 114
Thomas Edison, p. 164
Why Drew Was Late, p. 5

Honesty
Dare to Do Right, p. 172
Frederick and His Page, p. 208
Lessons from Washington, p. 161
Speak the Truth, p. 177
Terri and the Gooseberries, p. 130
Washington's Birthday, p. 163
Whole Duty of Children, p. 99

Humility
The Bird's Lesson, p. 170
The Eagle and the Mole, p. 178
Topknot, p. 139

Industry
A Cowboy's Day, p. 108
At Work and Play, p. 8
Birds' Nests, p. 34
Dare to Do Right, p. 172
Greta's Cow, p. 39
Our Flag, p. 18
Ruth in the Harvest Field, p. 187
The Camel, p. 192
The First Balloon, p. 200
The Pilgrims, p. 116
The Robins, p. 113
Thomas Edison, p. 164
Time To Rise, p. 99

Obedience
Lessons from Washington, p. 161
Terri and the Gooseberries, p. 130
Washington's Birthday, p. 163

Patriotism
Flags, p. 23
Looking for the Flag, p. 14
Our Flag, p. 18
The Army of Two, p. 70
Washington's Birthday, p. 163

Perseverance
Don't Give up the Ship, p. 49
The Camel, p. 192
The Good Shepherd, p. 77
The Pilgrims, p. 116
Thomas Edison, p. 164

Resourcefulness
The First Balloon, p. 200
The Four Musicians, p. 54
Thomas Edison, p. 164

Responsibility
A Cowboy's Day, p. 108
At Work and Play, p. 8
Dare To Do Right, p. 172
Frederick and His Page, p. 208
Greta's Cow, p. 39
Lessons from Washington, p. 161
Washington's Birthday, p. 163

Thoughtfulness/ Kindness
A Very Special Friend, p. 122
Frederick and His Page, p. 208
Helping Hands, p. 105
Lee and Traveller, p. 149
Ruth in the Harvest Field, p. 187
The Good Shepherd, p. 77
Whole Duty of Children, p. 99
Why Drew Was Late, p. 5

Uprightness
Dare to Do Right, p. 172
Frederick and His Page, p. 208
Terri and the Gooseberries, p. 130
The Lily, p. 83

through   pasture
dizzy   scampered

Muddy Mouse

Every day the Mouse family went for a walk.

When they came to a mud puddle, Father Mouse walked around it. Mother Mouse walked around it. Sister Mouse and Brother Mouse walked around it, too. But little Muddy Mouse walked right through it. He liked mud.

His friend, the horse, didn't like mud. The cow didn't like mud. The dog and the cat didn't like mud. But Muddy Mouse liked mud so much that he cried when there wasn't any.

One day Muddy Mouse played on the muddy pasture road. He rolled over and over down the road. Muddy Mouse thought it was fun, because the road was full of sticky brown mud.

But the mud stuck to his fur! More and more mud stuck to Muddy Mouse, until he looked like a big brown ball of mud. The tip of his tail stuck out of one side of the ball. The tip of his nose stuck out of the other side.

There was so much mud on Muddy Mouse that he couldn't walk. He couldn't talk. He couldn't even cry, and he wanted to cry very much.

Just then the black cat and her two kittens came along.

They thought Muddy Mouse was a big brown ball, so they started to play with him. They rolled him back and forth.

They rolled him around and around, until Muddy Mouse was dizzy.

Then the black cat and her two kittens gave Muddy Mouse a push. Away he rolled over the pasture. He didn't stop until he reached the fence.

After the black cat and her two kittens had scampered away, Father Mouse and Mother Mouse came out to look for Muddy Mouse. They looked under every stone and behind every bush.

But they would never have found Muddy Mouse at all if he hadn't wiggled the tip of his tail to call for help.

Then Father Mouse and Mother Mouse scraped and scraped and scrubbed and scrubbed at the big brown ball of mud.

At last they saw an ear, then a bright little eye, then a smooth gray back.

And after a long, long time there stood Muddy Mouse—all of him. He danced and squeaked with happiness, because he didn't have a single bit of mud on him.

Every day after that, the Mouse family still went for a walk.

And when they came to a mud puddle, Father Mouse still walked around it. Mother Mouse walked around it. Sister Mouse and Brother Mouse walked around the puddle, too.

But Muddy Mouse didn't walk around it. He *ran* around it.

Stop and Think

1. How did Muddy Mouse get his name?

2. How did Muddy get covered with mud?

3. How much of Muddy could be seen outside the mud ball?

4. Who came along to play with the mud ball?

5. Who found Muddy and what did they do?

6. Why didn't Muddy ever go through the mud again?

 minutes   hurry   trouble

Why Drew Was Late

Drew was on his way to school one morning, when he met a little boy. The boy was crying, and Drew asked what the trouble was.

"I can't find my way home," said the boy.

"What is your name, and where do you live?" asked Drew.

"My name is Alex Strong, and I live on Gray Street."

"Why, that is a long way from here," said Drew. "How do you happen to be so far from home?"

"I went for a ride on my bike and I rode too far."

"I think you did. I wish I had time to take you home, but I must go to school."

The boy began to cry again. "Oh, please take me home," he said.

"Oh, dear!" said Drew to himself. "I haven't been late this year. He should have gone home long ago." Drew stood still for a few minutes, and then went to Alex.

"I'll take you home," he said, "if you will stop crying. I don't like to walk with a boy who cries."

Alex stopped crying and began to smile. "You would have gone to school if I had not cried," he said, "and then I wouldn't have found my way home."

"That is so," said Drew. "Perhaps little boys like you may cry sometimes. You must hurry now, for I do not like to be late."

It was a long walk to Alex's home, but they reached it at last. Drew could hardly wait for Alex's mother to thank him and then ran as fast as he could to school.

He was ten minutes late, but when he told his teacher the reason, she said that he did what was right.

"But I wish I could have gone to school all this year without being late," said Drew.

Stop and Think

Would it have been right for Drew to leave Alex where he was just so that Drew would not be late one time all year?

The Bible Says,

"And be ye kind one to another . . ."

Ephesians 4:32a

precious

At Work and Play

A little play time does not harm anyone but does much good. After play time, we should be glad to work.

Travis liked a good game very much. He could run, swim, jump, and play ball; and he was always happy when the school bell rang and it was time to go home. But he knew that he could not play all the time. He knew that our minutes, hours, and days are very precious.

At the end of his play, he would go home. After he had washed his face and hands, and brushed his hair, he would help his mother, or do his homework, or read a book.

When he had done his work, he would play; but he did not try to play and to work at the same time. He used to say, "One thing at a time. Work while you work, and play while you play."

1. When is it all right to play at school?

2. What jobs can you do to help at home?

"And whatsoever ye do, do it heartily, as to the Lord, and not unto men."

Colossians 3:23

The Puppy's Day

It was morning. The puppy did not want to take a bath. Mary picked him up to put him into a bucket of warm water. He held on to Mary's hand. Mary could feel his heart beating very fast. He cried a little. "We'll be done soon," said Mary.

The puppy was:

    sad   angry   afraid   happy

After the bath Mary rubbed the puppy in an old towel. He ran away before he was dry. He barked at Mary. He pulled and shook her clothes. At last Mary caught him. "Keep still," said Mary.

Now the puppy was:

    tired   angry   afraid   playful

Mary put an old coat around the puppy. She rocked him in her arms. The puppy was still. After a while he opened his mouth. He yawned. He stretched. "Now, be a good puppy and go to sleep right away," said Mary.

The puppy felt:
   hungry   playful   sleepy   excited

In the afternoon Mary held up the collar for the puppy to see. He jumped up. He barked. He ran to the door and back again. He pulled at Mary's clothes. "Do you want to go? Go? Go?" asked Mary, as she put on her coat.

The puppy felt:
   sleepy   excited   tired   afraid

Mary walked to the corner with the puppy. There they saw another dog. He was very old. He turned to look at the puppy. He stood still. The puppy ran up to the old dog. The hair on  the old dog's back stood up straight. He growled. He snapped. "Puppy, come here this minute," called Mary.

The old dog felt:
    hungry   playful   angry   afraid

Mary walked fast. The puppy followed her. She ran along the sidewalk. The puppy ran to keep up with her. Out came his pink tongue. Mary ran again. The puppy began to pant. "Now it is time to go home," said Mary.

The puppy felt:
    afraid   sleepy   tired   angry

When they reached home, Mary went to the kitchen. The puppy followed her. He began to sniff. Mary put some milk in a saucer and set it on the floor. Sniff, went the puppy. Then out came his pink tongue. Lap, lap! He put his paws in the saucer. Lap, lap! Soon the milk was gone. "What a little pig!" said Mary.

The puppy felt:
   tired   playful   angry   hungry

That night Mary put an old coat in a big basket. The puppy jumped in. He turned around and around. He yawned. He sneezed. Then he curled up. Soon he was still. "Now, don't you move until morning," said Mary.

The puppy was:
   hungry   excited   sleepy   angry

janitor   officer   usual

Looking for the Flag

Jack went out one day to see where he could find his country's flag. He looked this way and that way, but he did not look up.

He passed a fire station. Two firemen were sitting out in front. "Is there a flag here?" asked Jack.

"Use your eyes," said one fireman.

"Look up," said the other.

Jack looked up to the top of the fire station. There on the long flag staff was a large red, white, and blue flag. "This is one place I have found the flag," he thought.

Next he passed his schoolhouse. The janitor was sweeping the sidewalk. This time Jack looked up. "I see the flag is up today," he said to the janitor.

"Yes, Old Glory goes to school every day," said the janitor.

"Now, I have seen the flag in two places," thought Jack.

Not very far from his schoolhouse was the police station. Officer Gray was standing in front of the station. Jack knew Officer Gray because he came every school morning to help the children cross the street.

Jack said, "Good morning, Officer Gray. I see that the flag is flying from the police station."

"Yes, Old Glory goes up every morning and stays until sunset," said Officer Gray.

"I have found the flag in three places," said Jack.

"In only three places?" asked Officer Gray.

Jack thought about what Officer Gray asked. There must be more than three places. There must be other places. "I will look for other places," said Jack to himself.

In the afternoon Jack's father took him for a ride in the car. They drove down to the river. A big boat was ready to sail. A large flag was floating from a pole at the back of the boat.

"There it is again," said Jack.

"What?" asked his father.

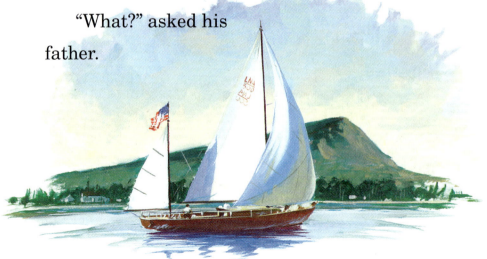

"Why, the flag," said Jack. "Old Glory is flying there on that boat. I have seen Old Glory four times today!"

That night Jack's father let him stay up a little longer than usual. Jack wanted to watch the news to see the space shuttle take off.

All at once, Jack saw it! There on the side of the shuttle was Old Glory—America's red, white, and blue flag.

Jack had a big smile on his face as he hopped into bed. He had seen the flag five times in one day.

 Stop and Think

1. What were the five places where Jack saw the flag?

2. Why was there a flag on each of these places?

3. Where else have you seen the flag of the United States?

4. Why do you think the flag is called Old Glory?

colonies	Vermont
needlework	Union
Kentucky	Declaration
Philadelphia	Pennsylvania

Our Flag

Our story begins on a warm, sunny morning in June 1777. In the little brick house at 239 Arch Street, Philadelphia, Pennsylvania, lived a young woman named Betsy Ross.

On this bright June morning everything was as neat and clean as Betsy could make it. General Washington had sent word that he was coming to call, to see about making a flag. On July 4, 1776, the American colonies had declared their freedom in the great Declaration of Independence. It was time this new nation had a flag of its own.

The clock in a nearby church had just struck twelve, when the commander in chief of the army and the famous banker, Robert Morris, were invited into Betsy Ross's home. Washington then took from his pocket a sketch of a flag.

"We are told," he said, "that you do the finest needlework in the city. Here is a drawing of a flag. It has thirteen stripes, seven red and six white, with a circle of thirteen white stars in a blue field. Do you think you can make the flag we need?"

"I am not sure, General Washington, but I will do my best to please you."

"I must ask you," continued Washington, "to make the stars as I have drawn them."

"But, General Washington, the stars in the sky seem to have five points, and your stars have six. Please allow me, sir, to show you what I mean."

With a single clip of her scissors she cut out a perfect five-pointed star.

"I have no doubt you are right," said General Washington. "You may make for us a sample flag as I have directed, but let the stars have five points."

Never did Betsy Ross do finer needlework, and her beautiful flag was accepted for the nation.

When Vermont and Kentucky came into the Union, there were fifteen stars and stripes. Later other new states were admitted, and new stars and new stripes were going to be added to the flag.

But the people did not like to have so many changes made in the flag.

"This will never do," they said. "Too many stars and stripes will spoil our flag."

So it was decided that after July 4, 1818, there would be only thirteen stripes, one for each of the first thirteen states. But when a new state was admitted into the Union, a new star would be added.

One by one new stars have taken their places, until today there are fifty in the field of blue.

Stop and Think

1. Who came to see Betsy about making a flag?

2. Why was Betsy Ross chosen to make the flag?

3. What kind of star did General Washington want?

4. What kind of star did Betsy Ross ask to be allowed to make?

5. How many stripes do we have in our flag today? What do they stand for?

6. How many stars do we have in our flag today? What do they stand for?

Flags

Annette Wynne

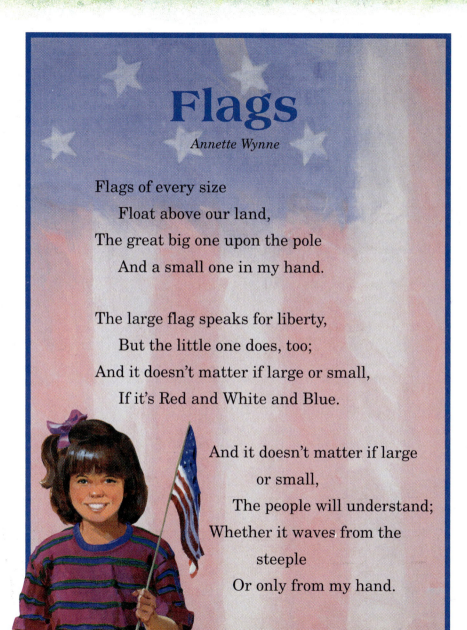

Flags of every size
    Float above our land,
The great big one upon the pole
    And a small one in my hand.

The large flag speaks for liberty,
    But the little one does, too;
And it doesn't matter if large or small,
    If it's Red and White and Blue.

And it doesn't matter if large
    or small,
    The people will understand;
Whether it waves from the
    steeple
    Or only from my hand.

Word Watch

danger   aquarium

The Sea Horse

There is a horse which lives in the sea. He is called the sea horse.

He is a tiny fish, not much longer than a child's finger. He is called a sea horse because his head looks like a horse's head. He holds up his head to look this way and that way just as colts do when they are getting ready to run.

The sea horse cannot run. Of course he can't. He has no feet. But he can go very fast swimming up on his tail.

Big fish try to catch him and eat him. He has to swim fast to get away.

When the sea horse gets tired, he does something that a horse cannot do. He ties himself. He winds his tail around the seaweed and rests while the water rocks him up and down.

When he is rested, he unties himself. Off he goes with his proud little head held high.

The father sea horse takes care of the babies when big fish try to get them. He has a pocket on the underside of his body. When danger is near, the baby sea horses get into this pocket to hide. When danger is over, out they pop again, looking this way and that.

Sometimes a few sea horses are brought to the city for children to see. They are kept in an aquarium which is filled with warm seawater, so that they feel at home.

 Stop and Think

Find the sentences that tell the answers.

1. What is the sea horse?
2. How long is he?
3. What gives him his name?
4. Why doesn't he run?
5. How does he rest?
6. Who takes care of the baby sea horses?
7. Where do the babies hide?
8. Where can children see them?
9. What makes the sea horse feel at home in an aquarium?

Rusty's Adventure

Once there was a small raccoon. His name was Rusty, and he lived in a grove of oak trees which grew in the middle of a big forest.

Lots of other animals lived in the oak grove with Rusty. There were moles, rabbits, chipmunks, groundhogs, owls, and even a small field mouse named Alice P. Dobbs.

The animals spent all their time in the shady grove of trees. They ate there, they slept there and they played games there.

They loved the oak grove. Rusty loved it too, but he wanted to go places and see things.

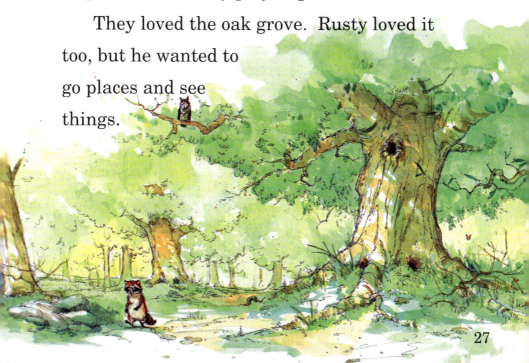

He said, "Nothing ever happens here. I'm going off to find a real adventure."

So he said good-by to the moles, rabbits, chipmunks, groundhogs, owls, and Alice P. Dobbs, and off he went.

Rusty looked for an adventure everywhere. He looked in caves, in trees, in nests, and in holes. But he couldn't find a single adventure.

Then one day, while he was walking in the forest, a large bee buzzed by. Rusty ran back to the oak grove as fast as he could go.

The animals were all there, playing "Ring around the Pine Cone."

Rusty shouted, "A bee chased me!"

The oldest owl shook his head. "*That's* not a real adventure."

The next day, while Rusty was walking in the forest, a huge bear trotted by.

Rusty ran back to the oak grove as fast as he could go.

The animals were all there, playing "Follow the Beaver."

Rusty shouted, "I heard a bear growl!"

The owl shook his head again. "*That's* not a real adventure," he said. Rusty felt very sad, but he decided to keep on trying.

The next day, while he was walking in the forest, a hunter went by. Rusty ran back to the oak grove as fast as he could go.

The animals were all there, playing "Chipmunk in the Dell."

Rusty shouted, "I saw a hunter!"

29

The old owl shook his head. "*That's* not a real adventure," he said. Rusty felt sadder than ever because he couldn't find an adventure, no matter how he tried.

The next day he went for a *very* long walk in the forest. He walked farther than ever before, and the farther he went, the sadder he became.

Soon he came to a road. On the road was a big truck. Rusty was very tired, so he climbed up on the truck and crawled in the back. Inside it was cozy and warm. Rusty sat there resting his paws quietly.

All of a sudden, the truck began to move. It went faster and faster! It went so fast that Rusty was afraid to jump off!

The truck drove until it came to a big city. Then it stopped, and the driver began to unload his boxes.

Rusty had never been so scared in his life. He jumped off the truck and began to run.

When the driver saw Rusty, he chased after him. Soon lots of other people began chasing him.

They chased poor Rusty all over the city. They chased him in and out of stores, through a park, and even into the subway!

Finally they caught him in a big net.

Everybody crowded around. A man took Rusty's picture. A dog barked. A policeman wrote things in a little book.

Soon another truck came. The driver put Rusty in a cage and put the cage on the truck. Then he drove out of the big city.

After a long ride, the truck came to the forest where Rusty lived. Then the driver opened the cage, and Rusty raced back to his oak grove.

The animals were all there, playing "Acorn, Acorn—Who's Got the Acorn?"

Rusty told them about his ride and all the other things that had happened. The animals listened, and their eyes grew wide with wonder.

The oldest owl smiled. He said, "Good news, Rusty! At last, you've had your adventure!"

Stop and Think

1. What kind of animal is Rusty?

2. Where did Rusty and the other animals live and spend all their time?

3. What things happened to Rusty that he thought were a real adventure even though they weren't?

4. Who told Rusty that these were not real adventures?

5. How did Rusty's real adventure begin?

6. Name 3 things that happened on his adventure.

Birds' Nests

What do you think is the best place for a bird's nest? Some birds build their nests low, and some birds build their nests high. Some put their nests in barns. Some build them in trees. Some make them on the ground.

This is a meadowlark's nest. The bird's name tells you where she puts her nest. It is on the ground hidden by the tall grass.

People walking through the meadow do not see the nest as it is loosely made of dry grass or hay. When the farmers cut their hay, they often find a meadowlark's nest.

True or False

1. The meadowlark's nest is on the ground.
2. It is made of mud.
3. It can be easily seen.
4. It is loosely made of dry grass or hay.
5. The farmer finds it when he cuts his hay.

In the country you often see a nest like this one. This nest was made by the barn swallow. You can see how the bird got its name. The nest is made of mud. It is put on the inside of barns or sheds.

The barn swallow finds a high place in the corner under the roof. This high nest makes a safe home for the young birds.

True or False

1. The barn swallow's nest is on the ground.
2. The nest is made of grass.
3. It is near the roof of the barn.
4. The barn swallow builds its nest in the city.
5. The nest is in a safe place.

Here is a nest in a tree trunk. This nest was made by the woodpeckers. The name tells you what they do. They work hard to build their nests. No bird works harder.

Woodpeckers go tap, tap, tap, with their bills. Soon a hole is made. It must be deep enough to keep the eggs safe from the owls.

The woodpeckers use their bills for shovels, too. They carry out all the chips so that the nest will be clean.

True or False

1. The woodpecker builds in a barn.
2. The nest is made of straw.
3. It is a deep nest.
4. Owls like the woodpecker's eggs.
5. The woodpecker's bill is strong.

Few people ever see a nest like this one. The eagle made this nest. It is built high among the rocks. It is so far away that men do not often find it.

The eagle's nest is made of sticks and grass. It is flat like a plate, and it is so large that a child cannot lift it.

True or False

1. The eagles build their nests among high rocks.
2. Many people find them.
3. The nests are made of sticks and grass.
4. They are very deep.
5. A child can lift an eagle's nest very easily.

Stop and Think

Where is it?

1. The eagle's nest is _____.

2. The woodpecker's nest is _____.

What is it made of?

3. The barn swallow's nest is made of _____.

4. The meadowlark's nest is made of _____.

Who makes it?

5. A low nest is made by a _____.

6. A nest in a tree trunk is made by a _____.

How do these birds learn where to build their nests?

Word Watch

guide
herdsman
milkmaid

Switzerland
friskiest

Greta's Cow

Greta was a little Swiss girl. Her father was a guide, her brother a herdsman, her sister a milkmaid, and her mother was the dearest mother in the world.

Greta had a cow of her very own. It was a present from her uncle who lived far away across the mountains. He had sent the cow by her brother Peter, with a message that pleased Greta very much.

"Tell Greta," her uncle had said to Peter, "that this cow is her own. She must learn to milk, churn, and make butter. When I come at Christmas to see her, I shall expect a pound of butter made by her own little hands for my Christmas gift."

You can imagine how Greta felt when she heard this. And her sister Rose promised to teach her how to do all these things as soon as the cows came home from their summer pasture.

Now in Switzerland, when the winter snows melt, the herdsmen take the cows to pasture high up on the mountains where the grass grows green and the cool winds blow. The milkmaids go to take care of the milk, and they stay in the highlands till the snow comes again in the fall.

Greta wanted her cow to go with the others, of course. So the very first night, after the cow came, Greta told her cow all about it.

"The cows will go to pasture very soon," she said to her cow, "and you will want to go, I know, so I will let you. You are my very own cow, but I will let you go where the little flowers bloom and the grass is green. Brother Peter says it is a wonderful place. You can see the snow on the mountaintop while you eat the grass on the mountainside. You must grow fat, too," said Greta, "and give a great deal of milk, for when you come back in the fall, I shall milk you myself."

The cow chewed her cud and switched her tail, but Greta knew by her eyes that she wanted to go.

It was a great day when the cows went to the pasture. All the cows in town went. They

wore bells about their necks and marched in a long line. Greta's cow had ribbons on her horns, and the little girl thought she was the prettiest cow in the whole line.

Greta watched the cows as long as they were in sight. Once her cow looked back and called, "Moo! Moo!" just as if she were saying goodbye.

"Goodbye," cried Greta.

"Goodbye," said Brother Peter and Sister Rose. And away they went, leaving Greta in the valley.

Summer was a busy time for Greta. She was her mother's chief helper when Sister Rose was away. There was always something for her to do. The days slipped by quickly. Greta was surprised one evening when her father came home and said, "I passed the cows on the road today. They will be here tomorrow."

"Tomorrow!" cried Greta with delight.

"Yes, tomorrow," said her father. "And your cow—" but he stopped and put his hand over his mouth.

"I can't tell. It is a secret," he said, when Greta looked at him in wonder.

"Oh, Father, Father, please tell!" begged Greta. "What is it about my cow?"

But her father would not tell. "I can't tell, even if you guess it," he said. "Brother Peter and Sister Rose said to me again and again, 'Don't tell Greta that her cow—'"

Greta could not keep from guessing. "My cow gives more milk than any other cow!" No, that was not it, she knew by her father's smile. "Her milk is the richest!" Still she was wrong.

"Oh, Mother!" she cried. "What do you think it can be?"

"I am not going to guess," said her mother, "because it is a secret. Perhaps you will dream it when you go to sleep tonight."

So Greta went to sleep and dreamed all night of cool pastures and green grass. But she could not dream what the wonderful secret was.

Early the next morning she went out and sat by the roadside. She waited and watched, waited and watched, until it seemed to her as if she could not wait another minute. Just about then she heard a sound far up the road.

Tinkle, tinkle! Greta knew what that meant. The cows were coming.

The leader cow stepped proudly in front. Then came her uncle's cows. They were very sleek and very fat.

The herdsmen nodded to the little girl. "Good morning, Greta," they said, and they smiled as if they knew the secret.

Then came her next-door neighbor's cows. He was with them himself, and he, too, looked at Greta. "Good news for you," he called as he passed.

"Oh! what can it be? What can it be?" cried Greta. "Will they never come?"

At last her mother's cows came slowly down the path. There were six of them, and they greeted Greta with their soft, loving eyes. "We know," they seemed to say, "but we cannot tell."

Greta almost held her breath. There came Sister Rose, and her Brother Peter, and her cow. Close behind trotted the dearest, loveliest, friskiest baby calf!

The secret was out, and Greta was the happiest little girl in Switzerland.

Stop and Think

1. Who gave Greta her cow?

2. What did Greta's uncle expect to have when he came at Christmas?

3. Why did the cows go to pasture for the summer?

4. What did Greta do during that long summer?

5. What was the surprise that Greta's cow brought back with her?

6. What job did each person in Greta's family do?

merrily   splendid
together noble
patient   brooklet

The Boy and the Wind

Marie Zetterberg

A boy one day
Went out to play;
'Twas in the bright spring weather.
The wind and he,
Right merrily,
Did often play together.

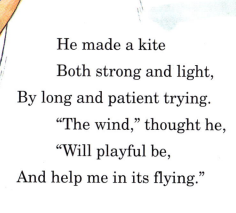

He made a kite
Both strong and light,
By long and patient trying.
"The wind," thought he,
"Will playful be,
And help me in its flying."

The wind came past;
The boy ran fast;
The kite rose high and higher.
Hard pulled the kite,
O splendid sight!
It was a noble flyer.

He made a boat
To set afloat
Upon a brooklet flowing;
The March winds blew
The meadow through
And kept the sailboat going.

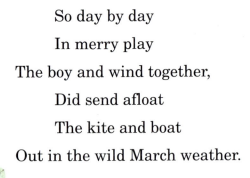

So day by day
In merry play
The boy and wind together,
Did send afloat
The kite and boat
Out in the wild March weather.

| disturb | rhyme | gallant |
| problem | annoys | disappoint |

Don't Give Up the Ship

Jared was talking to his sister one day. "Sara, what makes people say, 'Don't give up the ship'?"

"I don't know," Sara said. "That's what Mrs. Jennings said to me yesterday when I couldn't understand my math problem."

"Yes," said Jared, "and that's what Dad said to me. I told him I could never learn to write neatly. He only said, 'You must not give up the ship, my boy.'"

"I don't have a ship to give up," said Sara.

"And what does a ship have to do with my writing?" said Jared.

"There must be a story about a ship," Sara said.

"Maybe Grandfather would know," said Jared. "Let's ask him."

They found their grandfather writing a letter in the next room. They did not want to disturb him, so they turned to leave.

But Grandfather looked up just then. He smiled and laid down his pen. "Did you want something?"

"We wanted to ask you a question," said Sara. "We want to know why people say, 'Don't give up the ship.'"

"We thought maybe there is a story about it," said Jared.

"Yes, there is," said their grandfather. "And I know a little rhyme that tells the story."

"Could you tell us the rhyme?" asked Sara.

"Yes, if I can think of it. Let me see. How does it begin?"

Grandfather leaned his head back in the chair. He shut his eyes for a moment, trying to remember.

"Oh, now I remember it!" he said. And this is what Grandfather said:

> When I was but a boy,
>   I heard the people tell
> How gallant Captain Lawrence
>   So bravely fought and fell.
>
> The ships lay close together,
>   I heard the people say,
> And many guns were roaring
>   Upon that battle day.
>
> A grape-shot struck the captain,
>   He laid him down to die:
> They say the smoke of powder
>   Made dark the sea and sky.
>
> The sailors heard a whisper
>   Upon the captain's lip:
> The last command of Lawrence
>   Was, "Don't give up the ship."

And ever since that battle
    The people like to tell
How gallant Captain Lawrence
    So bravely fought and fell.

When disappointment happens,
    And fear your heart annoys,
Be brave, like Captain Lawrence—
    And don't give up, my boys!

 **Stop and Think**

1. Who told Sara "Don't give up the ship"? Why?

2. Who told Jared "Don't give up the ship"? Why?

3. Who knew the story about the saying?

4. In the poem, who was in charge of the ship?

5. How would Grandfather's poem help Jared?

 **The Bible Says,**

"Whatsoever thy hand findeth to do, do it with thy might."

Ecclesiastes 9:10a

Word Watch

musicians

The Four Musicians

"I can't work anymore," said a poor old donkey. "My master will not keep me. I will go to the city where I have heard the band playing in the streets. I can play in the band as well as anyone, for I have a fine voice."

The donkey had not gone far when he saw a dog lying in the road.

"Why are you here?" asked the donkey.

"I have run away from home," said the dog. "My master says that I must be killed because

I am too old to hunt. I do not know how I am to earn my living."

"Come with me," said the donkey. "I am going to the city to play in the street band. I can play the horn, and you can beat the drum."

"Thank you," said the dog. "I will come, too." And they went together.

Not long after, they came to a cat sitting by the roadside. She was looking as sad as three rainy days.

"Why do you look so sad?" asked the donkey.

"My master has turned me out of the house because I am too old to catch mice," said the cat. "I don't know where to go to find a home."

"Will you join our band?" said the donkey. "You have a good voice for night singing."

"Thank you," said the cat, "I will." And they all went together.

Soon they came to a farmyard. There sat a rooster on the gate crowing with all his might. "Why do you crow so loud?" they asked.

"I have heard the cook say that I am to be killed for dinner," said the rooster. "I shall crow as long as I can, for I'm afraid tonight I will lose my head."

"Why don't you run away?" said the donkey. "Go with us to the city. We shall be glad to have your voice in our band."

"Thank you," said the rooster. And they all went on together.

At night they came to a forest. "Let's rest here," said the donkey. "I will lie down under this tree."

"I will lie by your side," said the dog.

"I will climb the tree and sit on a large branch," said the cat.

"And I will fly to the top of the tree," said the rooster.

Before they slept, they heard a call from the rooster. "I see light," he said. "It must be in a house near by."

"Let us go and see," said the dog. "I would like to find a bone for my supper."

They all went on together until they came to a little house in the woods. A light was shining from a high window.

"I wish we could see into this window," said the dog.

"It is too high for me," said the cat.

"I have a plan," said the donkey. "I will stand under the window. Friend Dog, you get on my back. Cat, you may climb on the dog's back. Now, Rooster, you may fly to the cat's head and look into the window."

"What do you see?" asked the donkey.

"What do I see!" answered the rooster. "I see a table full of good things to eat, and robbers sitting round it."

"Can't we drive the robbers away?" said the dog.

"I know how we can do it," said the donkey. "When I count three we must all make a great noise."

"Ready, now," he said. "One, two, three." The donkey brayed, the dog barked, the cat mewed, and the rooster crowed. The robbers jumped from the table, and ran into the woods.

Then the four friends went into the house, and there they had a good supper.

The little house in the woods became their home, and if they have not moved away from it, they are living there still.

Stop and Think

1. What was the first animal that left for the city to play in the band?

2. What other animals joined him?

3. Why were they in a forest?

4. Who saw the light first?

5. Who was in the house?

6. What did the animals do?

| fussed | company | chorus |
| fretted | crowded | plenty |

A Cow in the House

Once there was a poor farmer. He lived with his wife in a little red house.

The little house had only two tiny rooms, and a tiny porch on the side.

The farmer and his wife thought their house was just the right size. Then one morning the farmer's wife made noodles.

The noodles were extra long, and the kitchen was extra short. And there the trouble began.

"If only we could buy a larger house," said the farmer's wife.

And she fussed and she fretted the whole morning long.

"We have no money to buy a larger house," said the farmer. So away he went to tell his trouble to Grandpa Wiseman.

"If you will do just as I tell you," said Grandpa Wiseman, "then everything will turn out all right."

"Indeed I will," said the farmer.

"First," said the old man, "you must take your hen into the house."

So the farmer went home, and he took his hen into the house.

The hen had never been in a house before. She did not know how to behave. She jumped up on the table and onto the farmer's lap.

At last the farmer could stand it no longer. He went to see Grandpa Wiseman.

Grandpa Wiseman said, "Now you must take the goat into the house."

So the farmer went home and took his goat into the house.

The goat ate the curtains. She slept on the bed. She smashed chairs. She fought with the hen.

So back went the farmer to tell Grandpa Wiseman about it.

"Both the hen and the goat need company," said the old man. "Now you must go home and take your pig into the house."

"Oh, no," said the farmer, "not the pig!"

"Yes," said Grandpa Wiseman, "the pig!"

The pig took up a lot of room. He was more trouble than both the goat and the hen.

Everywhere the farmer's wife tried to put something, there was the pig.

Besides, the hen and the goat and the pig did not get along well together. Back went the farmer to tell Grandpa Wiseman about it.

"You must take the cow into the house," said the old man.

So the farmer went home again.

The minute the cow got into the house, she sat down in the doorway. The farmer and his wife could not get out of the door to do their chores. With the hen and the goat and the pig taking up the rest of the room, there was nothing for the farmer and his wife to do but sit.

At last the farmer climbed out the window. He went to see Grandpa Wiseman.

"How are you getting along now?" asked the little old man.

"Well," said the farmer, "we're a little bit crowded. Still, it *could* be worse."

"How could it be worse?" said Grandpa Wiseman.

"Suppose my cousin and his wife and his ten children and their dog and cat should come and stay with us," said the farmer.

"Things would really be crowded then, wouldn't they?" laughed Grandpa Wiseman.

"Yes, indeed," said the farmer, "things can always get a little bit worse."

"Now we're getting somewhere with your problem," said Grandpa Wiseman. "Run home now, and push the cow out of the house."

"By all means!" said the farmer. He could hardly wait to get home.

It was simply wonderful having the cow out of the way. The farmer told Grandpa Wiseman about it.

"Fine," said Grandpa Wiseman. "Now drive the pig back into the pigpen."

"Yes, indeed," said the farmer, and he lost no time in doing as the old man said.

"Does your house seem larger now?" Grandpa Wiseman asked.

"Oh, yes," said the farmer. "We have lots and lots of room now!"

"Fine," said the old man. "Now it's time to drive out the goat."

Soon the goat was out in the yard again. The house never seemed so large.

"We are beginning to rattle around like peas in a pod," the farmer told the old man.

"In that case," said Grandpa Wiseman, "you can let the hen out."

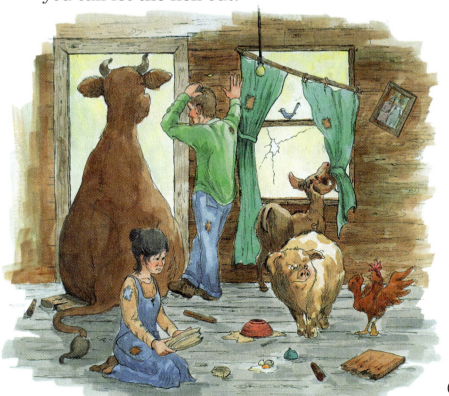

Now the little red house was just the right size for the farmer and his wife.

"I wouldn't want a larger house now," said the farmer's wife.

And away she went to the kitchen to make more noodles.

The noodles were still extra long, and the kitchen was still extra short. Still there was plenty of room in the little red house.

"It's all in knowing how to make the best of things," said the farmer. "And that's the truth!"

Stop and Think

1. Who thought the house was too small?

2. Who did the farmer go to for advice?

3. What animals ended up in the house?

4. Why did the house seem large enough once the animals were all pushed back outside?

5. What lesson was Grandpa Wiseman trying to teach the farmer and his wife?

The Two Buckets

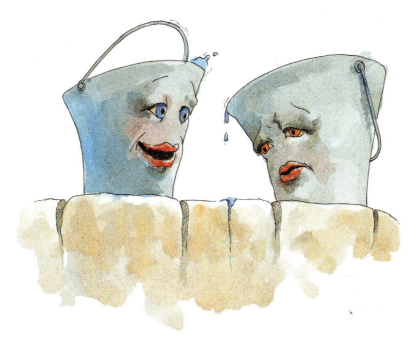

"How unhappy you look!" said one bucket to another as they were going to the well.

"Ah!" replied the other. "I was thinking how useless it is for us to be filled. No matter how full we are when we go away, we always come back empty."

"Dear me! How strange to look at it that way!" said the other bucket. "I enjoy thinking that no matter how empty we come, we always go away full."

| cunning | waterproof |
| dandelion | brooklet |

THE RAIN

Who likes rain?

    "I," said the duck, "I call it fun,

    For I have my little red rubbers on.

    They make a cunning three-toed track

    In the soft, cool mud as I pass.

      Quack, quack! I like the rain!"

Who likes the rain?

    "I," cried the dandelion, "I!

    My roots are thirsty, my buds are dry."

    And she lifted her shining yellow head

    Out of her green grassy bed.

      "I like the rain."

Who likes the rain?

    "I! And I hope 'twill pour, pour,"

    Croaked the tree toad at his gray bark door.

"With a broad leaf over me for a roof,
I feel that I'm quite waterproof.
　　I like the rain."
Who likes the rain?
　"I," sang the brook, "I like every drop,
And I wish the rain would never stop
Till a big, big river I grow to be,
Rushing along to the wonderful sea.
　　I like the rain."
Who likes the rain?
　"I," shouted Ned,
　　"for I can run,
With my high-top
　　boots and my rain
　　coat on,
Through every
　　puddle and brooklet
　　and pool
That I can find on my
　　way to school.
I like the rain."

harbor: quiet water where ships can anchor

fife: a small musical instrument, like a flute

Lieutenant: an American officer

The Army of Two

During the War of 1812 many great battles were fought. When the war was over, there was no story the people liked better to tell than the story of two little girls, Rebecca and Sarah.

Rebecca's father kept the lighthouse, and Sarah was Rebecca's playmate. One day when the children were at play they saw an English ship coming into the harbor.

Now Rebecca's father had gone across the bay, and the children were alone.

"What is that?" they cried, when they saw the ship.

"It looks like an English ship."

"But what is it doing in our harbor?"

"I fear it has come for no good," Rebecca thought.

Then the children ran up into the lighthouse to watch. Yes, it was an English ship, coming straight into the bay. It had already begun its mischief; for it had set fire to a little boat that lay outside the harbor.

"Oh, if I were a man, wouldn't I fight?" cried Rebecca.

"And I, too," cried Sarah.

The little girls watched and watched. What could they do? If they could only warn the people of the village! But they could not, for they had no boat.

"Couldn't we scare the English away?" they wondered.

"There is a drum in the lighthouse," said Rebecca.

"There is a fife, too. Let us go and get them!"

"I can beat the drum."

"And I can play the fife," said Sarah.

Then down the stairway the two children ran to find the drum and the fife. They would play them as hard as they could, and maybe the English would think an army was coming.

Then the children crept around behind the lighthouse and along through the bushes.

"Rat-a-tat, rat-a-tat, rat-a-tat-tat!"

"Trill-a-twee! Trill-a-twee!"

"Listen!" called the English captain.

"Rat-a-tat, rat-a-tat, rat-a-tat-tat!"

"Trill-a-twee! Trill-a-twee!"

"Troops!" said the soldiers. "But where are they?" Then they listened again. The music seemed to be coming nearer and nearer.

"They are coming along the point," said the captain. The soldiers scrambled into the ship and pulled up the little boats.

"The people have seen us. We will go away and try this port some other day," said the captain. Then they turned the ship and sailed out of the harbor.

"I believe they were really frightened at our music," said the children.

Meantime the people in the village heard the music too. What did it mean? Where did it come from?

As soon as the ship turned away, the village people hurried over to the lighthouse. And what did they find there? Only two little girls!

"Do you think we scared them away?" asked Rebecca.

"There can be no doubt of it," the people said.

From that time, as long as Rebecca and Sarah lived, they were called Captain Rebecca and Lieutenant Sarah. Sometimes they were called the American Army of Two!

Stop and Think

1. Which war is this story about?
2. What was Rebecca's father's job?
3. Who was Rebecca's friend?
4. Was anyone around to help them?
5. What did they use to scare the English away?
6. Whom did the English think they were?
7. How were Rebecca and Sarah brave?

Word Watch quarreling   untie

United We Are Strong

There was once an old man whose sons were always quarreling. If they played, cross words were heard. If they worked, each boy said that the other boys did not do their share of the work.

One day the old man told his sons to bring him some small sticks. These he tied closely together into a bundle.

"Now, boys," he said, "who can break these sticks?"

"Let me try, let me try!" said each boy.

One after another they all tried, but not one of them could break a single stick in the bundle.

"Untie the bundle and then see if you can break the sticks," said the father. They did so, and every stick was easily broken.

"My sons," said the old man, "if you will stand together, you will be strong like the bundle of sticks. But if you quarrel, each one of you will be weak like a single stick."

The Bible Says,

"If it be possible, as much as lieth in you, live peaceably with all men."
Romans 12:18

graze: to eat grass

cloak: a coat

crook: a long, narrow piece of wood with a hook on one end

bleat: sound made by sheep

The Good Shepherd

There was once a Shepherd who had a flock of one hundred sheep to care for. There were old sheep, and tiny baby lambs with such weak legs that the Shepherd had to carry them over the rough places in the road. There were black sheep and white sheep—a very large flock to tend. But the Shepherd was always kind and good.

Each morning he opened the sheepfold and led the flock over the mountain roads and beyond the hills to a wonderful green pasture. In this pasture the sun shone brighter, and the grass grew thicker, and the brook ran clearer than anywhere else. All day the sheep grazed, and drank from the brook, and lay under the shade of the olive trees. The little lambs played in the sunshine with no fear. The Shepherd was always quite close by to keep away the wild beasts that hid in the mountain passes. When night came he led the sheep home and watched through the dark while they slept.

But one day the sun forgot to shine. Thick, black clouds covered the sky. When the Shepherd gathered his flock to start for home in the

evening, the thunder began to rumble. A cold wind blew, and the blinding rain fell until it was hard to see the road at all. The Shepherd wrapped his cloak closely about him. He used his crook to push away the branches that the wind had torn off. He called softly to the sheep, each one by its name, for he knew them all.

They were nearly home when the Shepherd heard a low "baa, baa," close at his side. He stooped down to listen. A mother sheep was looking up into his eyes and trying to say something which he could not understand. The mother sheep kept tugging at the Shepherd's crook. Then she would back a little way and bleat again to tell him that something was wrong.

"Aren't my sheep all here?" asked the Shepherd. Then he went up and down the path, touching each one gently, and speaking its name, and counting: "One, two, three—" But there were only ninety-nine sheep in the flock.

The mother sheep had known. Her own little lamb was lost!

So the Shepherd turned back, leaving the ninety-nine sheep in the wilderness. He hurried through the dark and the storm to find the lamb that was lost. He was a good Shepherd. He knew that he could never lock the door of the sheepfold with one of the flock outside.

The rain beat into his face, and the stones and the branches caught at his feet. But on and on he went, up the mountainside, looking under every bush and in every hollow for the little lamb. There were no stars to light his way. The wolves came out of their dens to snarl and growl as he went past. But he whispered to himself in the dark,

> "What man of you, having an hundred sheep, if he lose one of them, doth not leave the ninety and nine in the wilderness, and go after that which is lost, until he find it?"
>
> –*Luke 15:4*

At last, when he had gone a long, long way, he found the smallest lamb of the whole flock. It was caught in some bushes by the side of the road. The lamb was crying because one of its legs was cut and bleeding. When the Shepherd found it, he laid it tenderly on his shoulder and covered it close with  his warm cloak. And "he went on his way, rejoicing."

The sheep were waiting for him, and they hurried together down the road. The Shepherd carried the little lamb all the way. They were tired, and wet with the rain, before they reached home. But just as the fold was in sight, the storm stopped and the stars shone out in the sky.

The good Shepherd opened the door of the fold and led in his flock. Then he called his friends and neighbors, saying to them, "Rejoice with me, for I have found my sheep which was lost!"

1. How many sheep were in the Shepherd's flock?
2. How did the Shepherd know that a lamb was missing?
3. What did the Shepherd do with the rest of the flock while he went to search for the lost lamb?
4. What did the Shepherd do after all one hundred sheep were safe in the fold?
5. What kindness did the Shepherd show?
6. Who is our Shepherd?

"I am the good shepherd: the good shepherd giveth his life for the sheep."

John 10:11

The Lily

W. T. Vlymen

The sweetest thing in
    my garden,
On bush or vine
    or tree,
Is the snow-white,
    shining lily
That God has sent
    to me.

How wise He must be
    to make it!
How good to put
    it here,
For me to watch
    and care for,
So very sweet and
    dear!

There's nothing more
    fair and spotless
In all the world
    I know;

It is fairer than the
    moonlight,
And whiter than
    the snow.

I love you, beautiful
    lily,
Made of the sun
    and dew;
I wish that my heart
    could always
Be spotless and
    pure, like you.

A Close Call

One bright summer day Dustin and Jamie went down to the beach to dig for clams. Dustin's little brown dog went with them. He watched the boys awhile. Then he trotted off to see what he could see. The boys called him "Pup," but Dustin was going to give him a better name some day.

Jamie looked after him.

"I wish I had a dog," he said. "But my mother says they eat too much. I had one once, but I had to give him away."

Dustin said, "He's pretty fine, all right. I wouldn't take twenty dollars for him. But never mind. I'll let you have part of him. So you won't need another dog."

When the boys had their pail full of clams, they ran to get their raft that they had made of some old boards. They pulled it into the water and began to float on it close to the shore. They had two small boards for oars.

"I'm going to be a sailor when I'm a man," said Jamie. "I like to be on the water. Don't you?"

Just then they heard a loud barking. The boys looked around quickly. They thought it was a strange dog. But no other dog was near.

"There's something white out on the water," said Dustin. "That's why Pup is barking. Let's paddle over and see."

As they hurried along, they could see a little girl's black curls and white dress come up and then go down again.

Dustin stood up on the raft and pointed to her.

"Go get it, Pup," he called to his dog, who stood barking on the shore.

The dog dashed into the water and swam to the place where the little girl had gone down.

Dustin and Jamie paddled as fast as they could. By that time Pup had a piece of the little girl's dress in his mouth. But he was not strong enough to pull her up.

It took only a minute for the raft to come up beside them. Both boys reached out. They pulled with all their might.

At last they dragged the little girl onto the raft, but she was white and still. Her pretty dress was soiled and torn.

"What shall we do now?" said Jamie in a hushed voice.

"We'll have to get someone to help us," said Dustin.

They pushed the raft quickly back to shore. Then they called to one of the cars that were driving along the road nearby. They ran and told the man and lady inside what had happened.

The man came and lifted the little girl into his car and drove as fast as he could to the hospital.

"I think she will soon be all right," said the lady as they waited in the room outside.

And she was right. The little girl was well in a short time; and the doctor phoned for her father and mother to come for her.

Her name was Kara. Her mother had told her many times never to go to the beach alone. But it looked so nice down there that she went anyway.

When her father came, he thanked the boys and said: "I am proud of you both. You knew what to do, and you did it quickly."

"We're glad we could help," said Dustin, "but our dog did the most."

"I must get something for him," said Kara's father. "What's his name?"

"We haven't named him yet," said Jamie, "but he's a fine dog anyway."

The next day a package came with a beautiful silver collar inside. On it was written "Fear-Not."

"That's what we'll call him," said Dustin, and everyone thought it was a fine name.

 Stop and Think

1. What was the name of Dustin's dog?

2. What were the boys doing at the beach?

3. Who saw Kara first?

4. How did the boys get help for Kara?

5. Why did the silver collar come the next day?

6. Why was Pup's name changed?

Word Watch

mistaken traveled

contented: happy with what you have

What They Found

Once upon a time there was a proud little hen. She lived in a barnyard with the other chickens, but she was not contented.

One day she hopped up on the fence and said, "I am going to look for the best thing in the world, and that is a big pile of corn. Yes, a pile of corn as big as a house."

Then the proud little hen jumped from the fence and started off. Soon she met a squirrel.

"Where are you going so fast?" he asked.

"I am going to look for the best thing in the world," said the little hen.

"What may that be?" asked the squirrel.

"A pile of corn as big as a house."

"Oh, no; you are very much mistaken," said the squirrel. "The best thing in the world is a pile of nuts as high as a hill. Come with me and we will look for it."

So the squirrel and the hen started down the road together. Soon they met a duck.

"Where are you two going so fast?" asked the duck.

"We are going to look for the best thing in the world," they said.

"And what may that be?" asked the duck.

"A pile of corn as big as a house," said the hen.

"A pile of nuts as high as a hill," said the squirrel.

"Oh, no; both of you are mistaken," said the duck. "The best thing in the world is a muddy pond as large as the ocean. Come with me and we will find it."

The three traveled together to the end of the road. It was a long and dusty walk in the hot sunshine.

They found no pile of corn, no pile of nuts, and no wide, muddy pond. So they turned around and started back home.

On the way they saw an old woodchuck eating supper by the door of his home in a hollow tree. He looked happy and contented.

"Where have you three been?" asked the woodchuck.

"We have been looking for the best thing in the world," they said.

"Why, you left it behind you early this morning," said the woodchuck.

"Where?" asked the three.

Then the woodchuck said to the little hen, "You left it in the barnyard."

He said to the squirrel, "You left it in the tree where your home is."

To the duck he said, "And you left it in your own duck pond."

"What was it?" cried the three.

"Contentment," said the woodchuck, as he took a big bite of apple.

1. What did the squirrel think was the best thing in the world?

2. Who wanted a muddy pond as large as the ocean?

3. What lesson did the woodchuck try to teach them?

Word Watch

speckled   soldiers   shadow
pleasant   Nanny

A Child's Garden of Verses

In a country across the sea there once lived a boy whose name was Robert. This boy knew how to make up games and plays and how to have a good time when he was alone.

He used to play in a garden near a great castle. There he climbed the cherry tree to look far away over the houses and the fields. There he heard the birds sing of speckled eggs and nests among the trees. And there he played with a funny shadow that followed him all about.

In his garden swing he went flying high in the air. He liked to look over the garden wall and down on the green grass.

One day he found a little pond with flowers growing all around it. He called this pool of water a sea, and he built a town upon its shore.

Sometimes he sailed his little ship on the pond. He wished that he were small enough to go to sea with the tiny captain that stood in the ship.

He played that he was the king of all the country around. The high grass he called a forest, and he watched the spiders and the ants go marching by.

In the evening Robert made plays from the stories he found in his picture books.

At night he called his bed a boat. He said "Good night" to his friends on the shore and sailed away to the town of sleep.

Robert had a Nanny whom he dearly loved. She played with him and read to him. When he could not sleep she carried him to the window to see the street lamps and the stars.

Robert was never a strong boy, and he spent many long days in bed. With his toys by his side he was happy all day long.

He called himself the giant of pillow-hill. He built cities with his blocks upon the bed and marched his toy soldiers all about.

Robert loved his picture story books, and he liked to tell stories himself. When he was only nine years old, he wrote a little book and drew all the pictures for it.

When Robert Louis Stevenson became a man, he wrote many books. But he never forgot the days when he was a little boy playing in the garden by his old home.

In beautiful verses he told of the games he used to play and of the story books he used to read.

These poems are put together in a little book for children to read. The book is called *A Child's Garden of Verses.*

Here are a few of those poems for you to enjoy.

Singing
Robert Louis Stevenson

Of speckled eggs the
    birdie sings
And nests among
    the trees;
The sailor sings
    of ropes and things
In ships upon the seas.

The children sing in far Japan,
    The children sing in Spain;
The organ with the organ man
    Is singing in the rain.

The Swing
Robert Louis Stevenson

How do you like to go
    up in a swing,
  Up in the air so blue?
Oh, I do think it the
    pleasantest thing
  Ever a child can do!

Up in the air and over
    the wall,
  Till I can see so wide,
Rivers and trees and
    cattle and all
  Over the countryside—

Till I look down on the
    garden green,
  Down on the roof so brown—
Up in the air I go flying again,
  Up in the air and down.

Time to Rise
Robert Louis Stevenson

A birdie with a yellow bill
Hopped upon the window sill,
Cocked his shining eye and said:
"Ain't you 'shamed, you sleepy-head!"

Whole Duty of Children
Robert Louis Stevenson

A child should always say what's true
And speak when he is spoken to,
And behave mannerly at the table;
At least as far as he is able.

The Cow

Robert Louis Stevenson

The friendly cow all red and white,
    I love with all my heart:
She gives me cream with all her might,
    To eat with apple tart.

She wanders lowing here and there,
    And yet she cannot stray,
All in the pleasant open air,
    The pleasant light of day;

And blown by all the winds that pass
    And wet with all the showers,
She walks among the meadow grass
    And eats the meadow flowers.

Rain

Robert Louis Stevenson

The rain is raining all around,
It falls on field and tree,
It rains on the umbrellas here,
And on the ships at sea.

Happy Thought

Robert Louis Stevenson

The world is so full of a number of things,
I'm sure we should all be as happy as kings.

Word Watch

miser wealth
pleasure neighbors

The Miser

Once upon a time there was a man who loved money better than anything else. People called him a miser.

All the money that he could get he put into a box. Then he hid the box in a hole at the foot of a tree in his garden.

Once every week he would get the box and open it and count his money. This gave him more pleasure than anything else.

One night some robbers got into the garden and found the box. They carried it away with all the money that was in it.

When the miser came, next day, to count his wealth, he found nothing there but the empty hole.

He was wild with grief. He cried out so loudly that all the neighbors came to see what was the matter.

He told them how he used to hide his money there and how he counted it every week.

"Did you ever make any use of any of it?" asked one of the neighbors.

"Oh, no; I only counted it," said the miser.

"Then you can still come and look at the hole. It will do as much good," said the neighbors.

Wealth that is not rightly used might as well never be.

1. Why was the man called a miser?

2. Where did he keep his money?

3. What did he do each week?

4. Why did the neighbors say that the empty hole would do him as much good as the money?

Word Watch

groceries

Helping Hands

Marcus was hurrying home from school one day. His friends were going to go sledding on Pine Hill.

He had his sled and was on his way to the hill when he saw Mrs. Hale. She was an older lady who lived down the street from Marcus.

She was carrying a big bag of groceries. There was so much snow and ice that she could hardly walk. Marcus ran past her with his new sled. He couldn't wait to try it out. "Hi, Mrs. Hale!" he cried as he ran past. But in a few moments he was back again.

He went to where Mrs. Hale was resting on some steps. "Good afternoon, Mrs. Hale," he said.

"I suppose it is a good afternoon for boys who like to sled," she said. "But I know I will slip on the ice."

"If you will put your bag of groceries on my sled," said Marcus, "I will take it home for you."

"What!" said Mrs. Hale. "I thought you were in a hurry to get somewhere. You ran past me so fast!"

"I am in a hurry to try my new sled at Pine Hill, but I can take your bag home for you."

So Mrs. Hale put the bag on the sled. Marcus had to go very slowly, because she couldn't walk fast.

One of the boys saw him and said, "Hey, Marcus! I thought you were coming to sled!"

Marcus laughed, and said, "So I am, but I am running an express now."

"Oh, I see," said the boy. "Well, I am going to the hill."

"I will be there soon," said Marcus.

When he came to Mrs. Hale's home he carried the bag into the house for her. "Thank you, Marcus," she said. "You are a kind boy."

"You're welcome," said Marcus with a big smile as he ran off to Pine Hill. And Marcus had the best time of any boy that day.

Stop and Think

Why did Marcus have more fun sledding on Pine Hill than any of the other boys?

Word Watch: freckles tomorrow

The Cowboy's Day

Danny was visiting Uncle Mack's ranch. There were six cowboys on the ranch. One of them was named Slim. He had red hair and freckles.

Danny asked Slim, "What does a cowboy do all day?"

Slim said, "You can ride with me tomorrow. You can see what a cowboy does all day."

The next morning Slim rode a white horse. Danny rode a spotted pony. Shep, the collie dog, ran with them.

"Where are we going?" asked Danny.

"We are going to drive some cattle to the mountains, where the grass is green," said Slim.

They rode over a hill. At the foot of the hill was a water hole. All around the water hole were white-faced cattle.

"Hey! Hey!" shouted Slim. "Get along there." Shep barked, and the cattle began to move away from the water hole.

The mountains did not look far away, but it was nearly dark when they got there.

"This is a good place for the cattle," said Slim. "It has plenty of grass and water. We'll camp here tonight."

Danny looked around. He saw a log cabin under the trees. They tied their horses under the trees and went into the cabin. In the cabin were a stove and a wood box, a table, and two bunks.

"This is a cow camp," said Slim. "When a cowboy is riding the range, he stops at a cow camp.

We keep something to eat here. We'll have a good supper tonight."

After supper, they took off their boots and went to bed. Shep slept under one of the bunks.

In the morning they had an early breakfast. Then they cleaned the cabin. Slim cut some wood, and Danny filled the wood box.

"Now everything is ready for the next cowboy," said Slim. "Today we will fix fences on our way back home." They rode away from the camp. Shep ran after them.

"What else does a cowboy do?" Danny asked.

Slim said, "A cowboy does many things. He takes care of his horses. He ropes calves and brands them. Sometimes he shoots a snake."

They rode slowly along the trail. They found several places where the fences were broken. Slim stopped to fix the broken places.

At the bottom of a hill Shep began to bark. Danny looked around. He saw some trees and a pile of rocks.

Danny called, "Slim! A little calf is caught between two big rocks."

Slim came quickly. He moved the rocks. The calf was free, but it could not walk. Slim ran his hand over the calf's leg. "No bones are broken. It was caught in the rocks so long that the feeling has gone out of its foot."

Slim pointed to the brand on the calf. "This is not one of our calves," he said. "It belongs to the Circle-A Ranch. We can stop there on the way home." He showed Danny how to carry the calf on his pony.

They rode until they came to the Circle-A Ranch. Dogs barked, and a boy ran out of the house.

"That's my pet calf, Trixie," said the boy. "Where did you find her?"

"We found her on our ranch," said Danny. "Her foot was caught in the rocks."

The boy took the calf in his arms. He said, "Thank you for saving Trixie."

Danny said, "Don't thank me. Thank Shep. He found the calf in the rocks."

Stop and Think

1. What was the first job that Slim and Danny did?

2. Where did they stay that night?

3. Why did they clean the cabin and fill the wood box before they left in the morning?

4. What job did they do as they rode home?

5. What did they find on the way?

6. What did Danny learn about being a cowboy?

The Robins

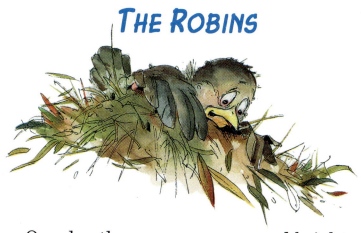

One day the sun was warm and bright,
   No cloud was in the sky,
Cock Robin said, "My little dears,
   It's time for you to fly."
And every little robin said,
   "I'll try, I'll try, I'll try."

I know a child, and who she is
   I'll tell you by and by;
When Mother says, "Do this, or that,"
   She says, "What for?" and "Why?"
She'd be a better child by far
   If she would say, "I'll try."

The Story of Barry: A Brave Saint Bernard

Barry lived with his masters in the high mountains of a very cold country.

Every day his masters would tie a small basket of food around his neck. Then they would send him out in search of people who had lost their way in the deep snow.

One day Barry found a man, half covered with snow, asleep on the side of the mountain.

Barry ran over to him and lay close beside him. The big, friendly dog licked the man's face and licked his hands.

By and by the man opened his eyes. How glad he was to see the friendly dog and feel his big, warm body!

Reaching over, the man untied the basket which was hanging from the dog's neck.

He was happy to find that there was food in Barry's basket. It had been many long hours since he had had anything to eat.

Barry took the man's cap in his mouth and ran away with it. He was going for help.

Before many hours had passed, Barry was back again with two of his masters.

The two men picked up the stranger and carried him to their home. There they kept him until he was well enough to go on his way. Barry had saved another life!

This brave Saint Bernard dog lived to be twelve years old. During his life he saved the lives of nearly fifty people.

Stop and Think

1. Who was Barry trained to help?

2. How did Barry help the man he found?

3. How many people did he save?

Mayflower   England
worship   Englishman
    Holland

The Pilgrims

Here is a picture of a ship called the *Mayflower*.

It came to this country more than three hundred years ago.

One hundred people came over in this little ship. They came to America to make new homes for themselves.

They did not wish to stay in England. Their king would not let them worship God as they wished.

So they left their own country and went to Holland. They called themselves Pilgrims because they went from place to place.

Soon they left Holland to come to America. They came in the *Mayflower.*

For many weeks this little ship tossed about on the rough ocean.

It was just before Christmas that the Pilgrims first reached the land. They thanked God for bringing them safely to their new home.

At first they built one big log house for all to live in. After a while they built a house for each family.

What a hard time they had! The winter was long and cold. Sometimes they did not have enough to eat. Many of them became sick and died before the spring came.

At first the Pilgrims were afraid of the Indians. One day they saw an Indian coming toward them.

They were ready to shoot him if he tried to harm them.

How surprised they were to hear him say, "Welcome, Englishmen!" They did not know where he had learned these words, but they were very glad to say, "Welcome, Indian."

A short time after this the Indian chief came and made friends with the Pilgrims. He brought other Indians with him. The Pilgrims and the Indians were friendly for a long time.

In the spring the Mayflower went back to England. The brave Pilgrims watched the ship sail away without them.

They had suffered very much and had been very sad at losing their friends; but they thought it was right to stay in the new land. So they would not give up and go back to their old homes.

In the summer they had good crops. In the fall they seemed to have plenty of food to last them through the next winter.

They said, "Let us thank God for our good crops." So they held a meeting and gave thanks to God. They had a great dinner too. Some of the Indians came to dinner. This was the first Thanksgiving Day in our country.

The Bible Says,

"In every thing give thanks: for this is the will of God in Christ Jesus concerning you."

1 Thessalonians 5:18

Thanksgiving

Elizabeth Coatsworth

The trees are red,

The fields are gold,

Once more the cow is in her stall;

The moon is large

And white and cold,

The geese fly south with their loud call.

Now is the time to gather in

The last bright apple from the tree,

For winter's cold

Will soon begin

Bringing the snow so white to see.

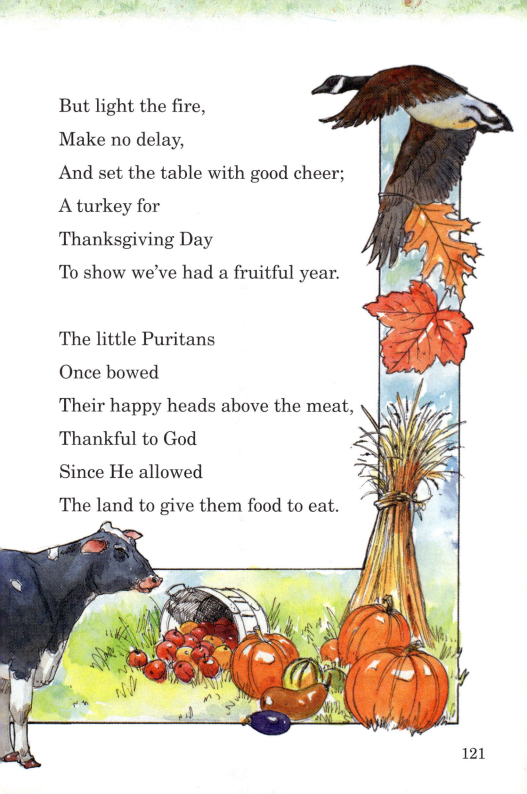

But light the fire,
Make no delay,
And set the table with good cheer;
A turkey for
Thanksgiving Day
To show we've had a fruitful year.

The little Puritans
Once bowed
Their happy heads above the meat,
Thankful to God
Since He allowed
The land to give them food to eat.

special	breath
language	leash
sighs	

A Very Special Friend

Abby was Jennifer's very special friend. It seemed like they were always doing things together. They loved to take walks, ride their bikes, or just sit and talk.

Jennifer could remember the day that she met Abby in Sunday school. She had seen how Abby watched Miss Shanks's mouth closely. Miss Shanks told the class that Abby had been quite sick a few years ago, and now she was deaf.

Even though she could not hear at all, Abby could still speak. She was also very good at reading lips and using hand signs called sign language.

After class, Jennifer had stood right in front of Abby and spoke slowly. "Hello, Abby," she said. "My name is Jennifer, and I want to be your friend."

"I'd like that!" Abby said as she gave Jennifer a big smile. "Do you know any sign language?"

"Just 'Jesus loves me,'" Jennifer said. "But I'd love to learn more. Can you teach me?"

"How soon can we start?" asked Abby with an even bigger smile.

The next Saturday, Jennifer had asked Abby to go to the park with her. They took Jennifer's dog Max along on his leash.

Max lay in the shade while the girls played on the slide, swings, and monkey bars. Then they played tag with Max. At last they fell on the grass, out of breath.

That was when they saw it. A small white kitten was curled up on a blanket asleep. Jennifer and Abby ran over to the kitten and started to pet it.

"Leave our kitten alone!"

Jennifer turned and saw two big girls running up to them. She jumped away from the kitten. But Abby couldn't hear the girls call out. She was still petting the kitten.

"Hey, you!" The biggest girl hit Abby's arm. "Get away from our kitten!"

Jennifer saw tears well up in Abby's eyes. "Please leave her alone," Jennifer said. "She's deaf. She didn't hear you."

Abby stood up and looked at the big girls. "This is a nice kitten," she said. Then she smiled at the girls.

The girls looked at Abby and then spoke to Jennifer. "Well, just stay away from our kitten and make sure you keep your slow friend away from it, too."

The girls made a face at Abby and walked off with the kitten.

Jennifer looked at Abby. Why did the girls think she was slow? Jennifer knew that she wasn't. Abby could run and play and think and talk just like she could. Abby was a sweet girl, and Jennifer knew that she loved Jesus, too. It was sad that some people did not understand.

The girls played on the slide and the swings some more. They ran and played with Max. Then while they were resting, Jennifer heard Max bark. He had slipped his leash and run off! She jumped up and grabbed Abby's hand.

Then they saw Max playfully chasing the little white kitten across the grass. The girls ran after them, calling out for Max to stop. They were glad the big girls were not in sight.

Just then Jennifer heard another sound. It was the tune the ice cream truck made! She had been waiting for the ice cream truck. Jennifer called to Max one more time as she ran over to get ice cream.

Max stopped running and went with Jennifer, but Abby kept running after the kitten. What she saw frightened her!

The kitten was running over a little hill right for the fence by the street. Trucks and cars were passing both ways. Abby knew she must catch the kitten before it scampered through the fence!

At that moment, the big girls came over the hill and saw Abby chasing the kitten. They watched as Abby scooped up the little kitten and held it close.

The girls came running up to Abby. Each girl had an ice cream bar in her hand. Jennifer came up behind them with two ice cream cones in her hands.

As soon as Jennifer got to where Abby was standing, she stood so that Abby could see her lips. "I'm so glad you got the kitten, Abby!"

The big girls did not know what to say. They knew that Abby had saved the kitten. She had stopped it right by the street.

Jennifer held out a cone to Abby. "Here," she said, "this is for you. When I heard the ice cream truck, I ran to get cones for us. I'm sorry I left you to chase the kitten alone!"

Abby handed the kitten to the biggest girl. "I'm glad I could save your kitten," she said. "If I had heard the ice cream truck, I might have left the kitten, too!"

The girls took the kitten. "Please tell her 'thank you'," the bigger one said to Jennifer, "and that I am sorry I said she was slow."

Abby smiled. "That's okay," she said. "Jesus helps me to be kind even when I don't feel like it."

The big girl stared at Abby. She did not know that Abby had been reading her lips! "What do you mean?" she asked.

"Jesus is my best friend," Abby said. "Jennifer and I learned about Him in Sunday school."

Jennifer said, "Maybe you can come sometime."

"Maybe we could," the girls said. They started walking with Jennifer and Abby. Jennifer saw that Abby had a big grin on her face.

Stop and Think

1. Where did Jennifer meet her very special friend?

2. What kinds of things do they enjoy doing together?

3. Was Abby deaf all her life?

4. How could Jennifer talk to Abby?

5. Who did the kitten belong to?

6. What special thing did Abby do for the big girls?

7. Why did Abby have a big grin when the girls were leaving the park?

clover   gooseberry
peering seriously

Terri and the Gooseberries

One day Terri went out to play with her pet rabbit. He was all brown, from the tips of his ears to the end of his tail, and Terri named him Mop. He had become as tame as a kitten, and Terri loved playing with him.

This morning, after she had given him his breakfast of apples and clover, she took him for a race in the garden. Mop scampered away after her down the path and hopped past her into the gooseberry bushes.

Terri ran after him and found him hiding under the leaves, peering out at her with his bright eyes. Just then, the gooseberries, which were full and ripe on the bush, caught Terri's eye.

"How nice they look!" she said to herself. "I'll just taste one. I won't eat it, because Mother doesn't like me to eat them." And she put the berry to her lips. It tasted so good that she thought she might as well swallow it. And then she thought two would not hurt her any more than one, so she ate two.

After that she ate another, and another, and then—

"Terri!" called her mother from the house. Terri jumped, swallowed the last berry whole, caught up Mop in her arms, and walked slowly into the house.

"What were you doing, Terri?" asked her mother.

"Oh," said Terri, looking all around the room, "I went out to play with Mop."

"Did you eat any gooseberries, Terri?"

"No, Mother, I didn't!"

"Theresa," said her mother seriously, "are you very sure of this?"

"Mother, look at Mop, how he is biting my finger. I don't think he's very polite, do you?"

"Terri, you did not answer my question."

"What was it about? Oh, I remember now. Yes, Mother, I am very sure of this."

"I hope," said her mother, looking steadily at her, "that my little girl will always be careful to speak the truth."

"Yes," said Terri quickly.

Terri's mother sat a minute as if she were thinking very seriously about something. Then she rose without another word and left the room.

As soon as Terri was left alone, she went into the corner behind the door and sat down on the floor. She sat there a long time, with her elbows on her knees and her chin in her hands.

It was the first time she had ever told a lie, and such a strange little pain had come into her heart that she thought at first she was sick, and she was quite frightened. But after a few minutes she began to understand that it was because she had done wrong. Then all at once she thought about God and knew that He would be saddened by her lie. And then she began to cry.

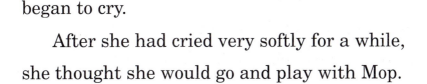

After she had cried very softly for a while, she thought she would go and play with Mop.

So she ran away and tried to play. But somehow, all the fun seemed to have gone out of everything. Besides, Mop made her think of the gooseberries; so she went back to her corner behind the door again and stayed there until lunch time. Then she skipped into the dining room singing some merry little song.

About the middle of the afternoon, Terri came into her mother's room, looking very serious.

"What is the matter?" asked her mother.

"Mother, I've been thinking that this is a strange world—don't you think so?"

"What made you think that, Terri?"

Terri began to play with the baby just then and didn't answer. After a while, she put her arms around her mother's neck and said, "I've got a stone in my heart, Mother."

"What do you mean, Terri?"

"Here," said Terri putting her hand under her chin. "I think I'm sick."

"My little girl is not very happy—isn't that it?"

"I am sad, but I think it's a stone. I must have swallowed it sometime."

"No, I don't think so," said her mother. "You want to tell me something, don't you?"

"Mother," said Terri in a tiny whisper, "what *do* you suppose I did?"

"What was it, Terri?"

"I—I ate a gooseberry this morning."

"I am very sorry to hear that," said her mother, laying down her work.

"I believe I ate two."

"Is that all, Terri?"

"I guess I ate a lot," said Terri, winking very hard to keep from crying.

"Why didn't you tell me that this morning?" said her mother sadly.

Terri hung her head.

"Thank you for finally telling me the truth, Terri. Taking the gooseberries was wrong, but lying about it makes it much worse!"

"Oh, Mother!" and Terri broke out in a sudden cry. "Oh, Mother, I am so sorry! I'll never, never do it again."

"I hope you won't, Terri," said her mother, "and now, because you disobeyed and ate the gooseberries, you must go to your room till supper time. And because you told a lie, there will be no dessert for you tonight."

It was a long and dreary afternoon to Terri as she sat alone thinking about what she had done. And it was very hard to just sit quietly while the rest of the family ate their dessert after supper. I doubt if she ever forgot it as long as she lived.

Stop and Think

1. Terri's pet rabbit was named _____.

2. Terri fed him _____ and _____ for breakfast.

3. *True or False:* Terri lied to her mother about the gooseberries.

4. Who did Terri know would be sad because of what she had done?

5. How could Terri have kept from eating so many gooseberries?

6. It would have been hard for Terri to tell her mother the truth at the very beginning, but it was even harder at the end. Why was this so?

7. *True or False:* Terri was punished for what she had done.

The Bible Says,

"For my mouth shall speak truth."
Proverbs 8:7a

Rabbits
Nancy Byrd Turner

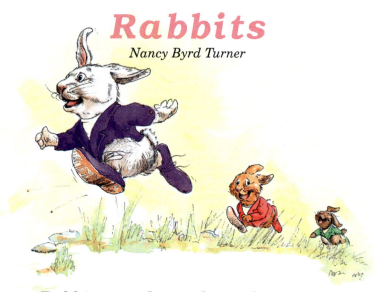

Rabbits are dressed in velvet coats
    And quiet velvet shoes,
And just as fast as wind they run,
    As often as they choose.

A rabbit sitting by a bush
    Feels rain upon his nose,
And suddenly decides to go—
    And up, away, he goes!

Across a field, and down a hill,
    And through green meadow ground,—
It must be fun to run, run, run,
    And never make a sound!

Word Watch   Topknot   shabby

Topknot

"Cluck, cluck, cluck!" said Topknot. "I am much too fine for this place!" She was walking in the barnyard.

"Cluck, cluck, cluck, what did you say?" asked the Rooster.

"I am going over the fence to walk by myself," said Topknot. "Just look at those shabby old hens! How they love that dust-heap!"

The Rooster shook himself and cried, "Go-go-go not there!"

And all the old hens cackled, "Go-go-go not there!"

But Topknot would do as she pleased. So she began to cry, "Cluck, cluck, cluck, over the fence! Cluck, cluck, cluck, over the fence!" And over she went.

She walked down the road to show herself off. How proud she was!

Just then a hawk began to fly above her. Suddenly he caught her.

When the Rooster saw that the hawk had caught Topknot, he cried out with all his might. "Come, come, come and help! Come, come, come and help!" he said.

All the people came running to see what was the matter. This frightened the hawk so much that he let Topknot go.

She was glad indeed to get away, and lost no time in running home. When she was safe in the farmyard again, she looked herself over. Her lovely topknot was gone.

Then she began to cry, "See, see, see how I look! See, see, see how I look!"

Up came the Rooster and made a low bow. "What did I tell you?" said he.

From that time, Topknot was very glad to walk on the dust-heap with the other hens.

Stop and Think

1. Why did Topknot think that she was too good for the barnyard?

2. What is it called when you think more highly of yourself than you should?

3. What happened to Topknot because of her pride?

The Bible Says,

"Pride goeth before destruction, and an haughty spirit before a fall."

Proverbs 16:18

lumbered waddled
tangled patiently
gnaw disappeared

Dapple Grey's Friends

Dapple Grey was frisking about in the barnyard. He caught his foot in a rope that was tied to an old post. He stumbled and fell. The more he tried to pull out his hoof, the more tangled it became. Though he kicked and pulled, he could not free himself, and at last he had to lie still and wait for help.

By and by Brown Cow came by and asked, "What is the matter, Dapple Grey?"

"I have caught my hoof in this rope, and I can't get it out," answered Dapple Grey.

"That is certainly too bad," said Brown Cow. "I feel very sorry for you, indeed." Then Brown Cow walked on.

Presently along came Big Pig and said, "What is the matter, Dapple Grey?"

"I've caught my hoof in this rope, and I can't get it out," answered Dapple Grey.

"Well, well, well!" grunted Big Pig. "I *am* sorry. I wish I could do something for you." Then Big Pig lumbered off.

Soon Black Dog came romping by. "Why, what is the matter, Dapple Grey?" he asked.

"I've caught my hoof in this rope, and I can't get it out," answered Dapple Grey.

"Too bad, too bad," said Black Dog. "It must be hard to lie there so long." Then away scampered Black Dog.

Next White Cat came walking softly by. "What can be the matter with you, Dapple Grey?" she asked.

"I've caught my foot in a rope, and I can't get it out," answered Dapple Grey.

"That must be painful," answered White Cat. "I'm sure I never could bear it as patiently as you do." Then she softly and lightly disappeared.

After a while Red Rooster strutted by. "What in the world is the matter with you, Dapple Grey?" he asked.

"I caught my hoof in a rope, and I can't get it out," answered Dapple Grey.

"That certainly is too bad!" crowed Red Rooster. "Isn't there anybody to help you?" Then, without waiting for an answer, he flapped his wings and strutted off.

Soon White Duck appeared, saying, "What is the matter with you, Dapple Grey?"

"I've caught my hoof in a rope, and I can't get it out," again answered Dapple Grey.

"Such a pity!" answered White Duck. "Such a great pity! I certainly wish I could help you," and she waddled off.

Dapple Grey was sad. "What will become of me?" thought he.

Just then a gray mouse poked his head up by the old post. He said nothing, but his bright eyes at once saw the trouble that Dapple Grey was in. He began to gnaw the rope with his sharp teeth—first one strand, then another, then another. Soon the strong strands gave way, and Dapple Grey's foot was free.

Dapple Grey jumped up quickly and turned to thank Gray Mouse, but Gray Mouse disappeared faster than he had come. "He shall have as much of my grain as he wants after this," said Dapple Grey.

Stop and Think

1. Why did Dapple Grey need help?

2. Which animals came by but did not help?

3. Who helped Dapple Grey?

4. Did Gray Mouse stop to be thanked?

5. Which animal would you like for a friend? Why?

The Bible Says,

"As ye would that men should do to you, do ye also to them likewise."

Luke 6:31

thicket: a thick growth of trees or shrubs

glossy: shiny

Old Mrs. Cricket

Old Mrs. Cricket,
Down in a thicket,
Brought up her children nine—
Odd little chaps,
In glossy black caps
And brown little suits so fine.

"My children," she said,
"The birds are abed;
Go and make the dark earth glad;
Chirp while you can!"
And then she began,
Till, oh, what a concert they had!

They hopped with delight,
They chirruped all night,
Singing, "Cheer up! cheer up! cheer up!"
Old Mrs. Cricket,
Down in the thicket,
Sat awake till dawn to hear.

"Nice children," she said,
"And very well bred;
My darlings have done their best.
Their naps they must take;
The birds are awake,
And they can sing all the rest."

mane   whistle

Lee and Traveller

Robert E. Lee loved horses. He had a fine horse named Traveller. Traveller was gray with a black mane and tail. General Lee liked to ride Traveller.

One day when Lee was out riding on Traveller he stopped to see a friend. The General tied Traveller at the gate and went into his friend's house. While he was in the house something frightened Traveller.

The frightened horse broke loose and ran down the road as fast as he could go.

Several men and boys tried to stop him. "Whoa, whoa, Traveller!" they cried. "Whoa, there!" But Traveller would not stop.

General Lee heard the noise and ran out of the house. He asked the men and boys to stand still. Then he gave a loud whistle. Traveller turned and came back to his master.

Everyone laughed. No one had had any idea that Traveller would come back. General Lee smiled and said, "Traveller always comes when I whistle."

When Lee was away from home, he did not forget Traveller. In one letter he wrote, "Tell the boy who takes care of Traveller to be very kind to him. Traveller should have his gray coat cleaned every day. Tell the boy not to pull his mane or tail."

Robert E. Lee was a great general

as well as a good man and a kind gentleman. He was known and loved by many people in this country.

1. What color was General Lee's horse?

2. Why did Traveller come when General Lee whistled?

3. How do you know that General Lee loved Traveller?

breathe   orchard

A Butterfly's Story

Once I was a little caterpillar. Then my home was on the apple tree in the corner of the orchard.

No home could be prettier than mine was. The sun shone through the leaves, and the soft wind rocked me to sleep.

I had a strange-looking body that was brown with black spots on it. There was a large white spot on my back.

I did not breathe as boys and girls do, but through little holes in my sides. I ate the leaves of the apple tree and grew very fast. I was soon too large for my skin.

What do you think happened then? My skin split open down the back, and there was a bright new one underneath.

I had four new dresses in this way. Each time the colors were different. Then I stopped eating.

By and by I fastened myself to a twig and shook myself out of my skin once more. This time, instead of a new skin, there was a hard shell over my body.

The tree rocked gently and I went to sleep. I think I must have slept a long time.

When I awoke, I made a little hole in the end of my shell and peeped out. I saw the green leaves and pretty blossoms.

I came out a little farther and looked around. There was the same old apple tree. The same bright sun was shining.

I crawled out and stood on a brown twig. How very strange I felt! I was not a crawling, creeping thing any more, but a beautiful butterfly.

My wings are yellow and black. I have six legs, and on my head there are two long horns or feelers. I take my food through a long tube, which is curled up out of sight when I am not eating.

On pleasant days you may see me flitting about among the flowers and trees. What a jolly life I lead! Who would not be a happy butterfly?

Stop and Think

What happened to the butterfly?

1. First he was a __?__ in an apple tree.

2. Then he shed his __?__ several times.

3. Soon his skin became a __?__ __?__, and he slept for a long time.

4. When he awoke, he was a beautiful yellow and black __?__.

Why Does the Breeze Blow?

Why blows the breeze so sweet?
It plays among the flowers
That blossom at your feet.

Why bloom the flowers so fair?
They love the shining sun,
And in his beauty share.

Why shines the sun so bright?
It hears the voice of God,
Saying, "Let there be light."

dirtiest   gravel

Fifteen Bathtubs

Once there was a little boy who lived in a house with fifteen bathtubs in it. You might think that this little boy was the cleanest little boy in the world, with fifteen bathtubs. But he wasn't.

He was the dirtiest little boy in the world. He hated to wash and he never used even one of the fifteen bathtubs.

Of course, he did take a bath once a month. But when he did take a bath, he used the garden hose. This dirty boy would run right through the water from the hose. That was the only way he took a bath, except when he took a sun bath.

He never got into one of the fifteen bathtubs.

One morning the little boy got up from the breakfast table, where he had been eating jam on toast. He wiped the jam across his face with the back of his hand. Then he went out into the garden.

Now this was a clean, shining morning. All the animals were out in the warm sun.

The rabbits hopped about, and the squirrels hopped about. The butterflies flew, and the bees went buzzing all around.

So the little boy lay down to take a sun bath. He turned his jam-sticky face up to the sky and closed his eyes.

The bees buzzed in the flowers. They flew through the air looking for something sweet to make into honey. Then they found the little boy's jam-sticky face.

The little boy was asleep. Bzzzzzzzz. A sticky treasure!

Suddenly many bees were flying all around the little boy's face. Zoom. Szzzz. They buzzed about his nose and lips. Bzzzzz. They buzzed nearer to his cheek. Szzzzz. Buzzz. They were after the sticky, sweet jam on his face.

The little boy jumped awake and he jumped to his feet and he jumped away. But the bees came buzzing all around right after him, trying to get the jam.

He ran and he ran, but still the bees came buzzing after him.

He ran all around the garden, and the bees buzzed all around the garden after him.

He ran and he ran into a field, and the bees buzzed through the field after him.

He ran and he ran and he ran through a wood, and the bees came buzzing after him.

Then he ran and he ran down the black tar road. The bees buzzed down the black tar road after him.

He ran and he ran up the gray gravel driveway. The bees came buzzing up the gray gravel driveway after him.

When he got to his house, he ran in the open front door. The bees came buzzing in the open front door after him.

He ran up the stairs, and the bees came buzzing up the stairs after him.

When he got to the fifteen bathrooms, he jumped into one bathtub
    and into another bathtub
        and another bathtub
        and another bathtub
        and another bathtub
        and another bathtub

and another bathtub

and another bathtub.

He jumped fifteen times, into all fifteen bathtubs.

Then the bees flew out the window and back to the flowers in the garden. They never chased the little boy again.

From that day on, he was just as clean as the sunlight.

Stop and Think

1. How often did the little boy take a bath?

2. Did he use a bathtub?

3. What was on the boy's face that attracted the bees?

4. Where did the bees follow the boy?

5. What lesson did the boy learn?

conduct: how a person acts

Lessons from Washington

When George Washington went to school, he studied reading, writing, and arithmetic. His written work was very neat and well done, and his writing books can still be seen in his old home at Mount Vernon.

One of the first lessons Washington learned was to obey his father and mother. He also learned to control his temper, to think before speaking, and to be true to every promise he made.

His father and mother taught him to be kind and polite to everybody. In one of his writing books he wrote fifty rules for good conduct. Here are some of these rules:

Always speak the truth.

Obey your father and mother.

Think before you speak.

Always keep your promises.

Always do your best.

Washington's Birthday

In honor of truth and right,
In honor of courage and might,
  And the will that makes a way;
In honor of work well done,
In honor of fame well won,
In honor of Washington,
  Our flag is floating today.

electricity   bamboo
        journey

Thomas Edison

Thomas Edison was a boy who always wanted to know "why."

He wanted to know why it rained and why it snowed. He wanted to know why animals eat grass and why people do not. He wanted to know why the trees drop their leaves every fall and get new ones in the spring.

Thomas Edison went on asking "why." Sometimes people would say "I don't know."

Then Thomas would ask, "Why don't you know?" But he did not mean to be rude.

When Thomas grew older, he began to ask about electricity. In those days, not much was known about electricity. The people he asked about it often answered, "I don't know."

Then Thomas began to read books to find out about electricity. But even the books did not tell him all he wanted to know.

Thomas kept on thinking about electricity. He hoped that someday he might find out all about it for himself.

One day Thomas was able to save a little boy's life by pushing him out of the way of a train. The boy's father wanted to thank Thomas for saving his son's life, so he promised to teach Thomas all he could about electricity.

Each day Thomas learned more and more about electricity. In those days, people did not have electric lights. When Thomas grew older, he tried to make an electric light.

Mr. Edison was busy day and night at his work bench. He tried over and over to make an electric light. He would not give up.

At last, Edison found that he could use bamboo cane to make a light. Bamboo is a tall plant that grows on the other side of the ocean. There are many kinds of bamboo cane.

One day Edison sent for one of the men who worked in his workshop. "Can you start on a journey around the world tomorrow?" asked Edison.

"Yes," replied the man. "How long will I be gone?"

"I don't know," said Mr. Edison. "You may be gone one year or it may even take five years. I want you to bring back all the different kinds of bamboo that you can find. Will you go on such a long journey?"

"Yes," answered the man, "I will go."

About a year later, the man came back from his journey, bringing home with him about a hundred different kinds of bamboo cane.

Edison used some of this cane to make an electric light. He used the bamboo to make the part which burns. When this was done, he turned on the electricity. His men stood by and watched.

"It makes a good light," said one of the men. "It will be a great blessing to us all."

"I can see on the other side of the room. It is wonderful!" said another.

The men all wanted to see how long the light would burn. Mr. Edison and his men watched the new light for three days and three nights without going to bed. At the end of that time, the little light was still burning.

"It is a good light," said Mr. Edison. "We need not be afraid that it will go out. There will soon be lights like this all over the world."

Thomas Edison kept on working, and almost every year he made a new electric light. Each one he made was a little better than the one before. Now, because of Mr. Edison's work, people have electric lights in their houses.

Edison kept on learning more and more about electricity. He found out how to send it from one city to another.

Thomas Edison could use electricity in more ways than any other man who had ever lived. All over the world he was known as a wise man.

From far and near people came to talk with him about his work. They wanted to learn about electricity from the man who wanted to know "why."

Stop and Think

1. Why couldn't Thomas learn about electricity when he first tried?

2. How did Thomas finally get to learn about electricity?

3. What did Thomas finally find that worked very well to make the electric light?

4. How did the people of the world feel about Thomas's work?

5. Why didn't Thomas give up after several tries?

The Bible Says,

"And whatsoever ye do, do it heartily, as to the Lord, and not unto men."

Colossians 3:23

Gracie   unnoticed

The Bird's Lesson
George Macdonald

A little bird, with feathers brown,
   Sat singing on a tree;
That song was very soft and low,
   But sweet as it could be.

And all the people passing by,
   Looked up to see the bird,
Whose singing was the sweetest
   That ever they had heard.

But all the bright eyes looked in vain,
   For birdie was so small;
And with a modest dark brown coat,
   He made no show at all.

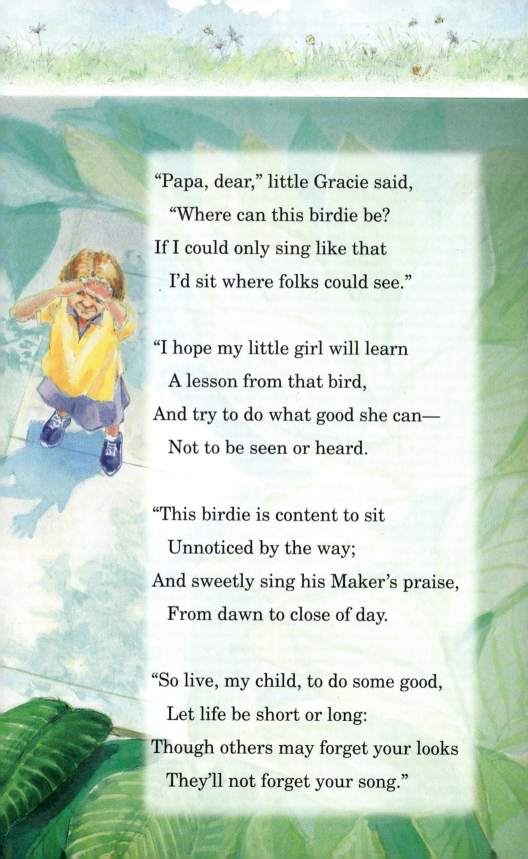

"Papa, dear," little Gracie said,
  "Where can this birdie be?
If I could only sing like that
  I'd sit where folks could see."

"I hope my little girl will learn
  A lesson from that bird,
And try to do what good she can—
  Not to be seen or heard.

"This birdie is content to sit
  Unnoticed by the way;
And sweetly sing his Maker's praise,
  From dawn to close of day.

"So live, my child, to do some good,
  Let life be short or long:
Though others may forget your looks
  They'll not forget your song."

terrified   startled

fierce

radiant: bright, shining

Dare to Do Right

A group of boys stood on the walk before a fine large drugstore, throwing snowballs at each other. Without meaning to do it, the youngest sent a ball spinning through the frosty air against the druggist's window.

The crash terrified them all, but none of them so much as the boy who now stood pale and trembling, with startled eyes, looking at the broken window.

"Won't Mr. Kendrick be mad? Run, Nathan! We won't tell. Run, quick!" said the boys.

"I can't," he gasped.

"Run, I tell you. He's coming!" shouted a boy.

"Coward! Why don't you run?" asked another.

"I guess he wouldn't catch me! Little fool! You'll be caught!" said one.

"Not strong enough to run away! Well, I've done all I can for him," muttered the oldest boy.

Just then, the door opened, and an angry face appeared.

"Who did this?" asked the owner in a fierce tone. "Who did this? I say," he shouted. No one answered. The trembling, shrinking boy drew near and faced the angry man. In tones of truth he replied, "I did it."

"And you dare to tell me of it?" he said as he caught Nathan by the collar of his shirt.

"I can't deny it; I can't tell a lie."

The reply was unexpected. The stern man paused. He saw the pale cheek and the frightened eyes, and his heart was touched. "Come here. What is your name?"

"Nathan Howe. Oh, what can I do to pay you? I'll do anything—" his eyes filled with tears, "—only don't make my mother pay it."

"Will you shovel my walk when the next snow falls?"

Nathan's face was radiant as he answered, "All winter. I'll do it every time, and more, too. I'll do anything."

"Well, that's enough. And do you know why I let you off so easy? It's because you're not afraid to tell the truth. I like a boy that tells the truth always. When the next snow falls be sure you come to me."

"Yes, sir, I will!"

"We'll all help him," shouted the others. And as they turned away, three hearty cheers were given for Mr. Kendrick, and three more for the boy that dared not to run away.

Stop and Think

1. What were the boys doing when the window got broken?

2. Who immediately wanted to tell the truth?

3. Was telling the truth easy?

4. What did all the other boys want Nathan to do?

5. Was Mr. Kendrick angry about his broken window?

6. What made Mr. Kendrick change his mind about being angry?

7. Why did all the boys cheer for Mr. Kendrick?

8. Why did all the boys cheer for Nathan?

The Bible Says,

"These are the things that ye shall do; Speak ye every man the truth to his neighbour."

Zechariah 8:16

Speak the Truth

Speak the truth!
Speak it boldly, never fear;
Speak it so that all may hear;
In the end it shall appear
Truth is best in age and youth.
    Speak the truth.

Speak the truth!
Truth is beautiful and brave,
Strong to bless and strong to save;
Falsehood is a cowardly knave;
From it turn thy steps in youth—
    Follow truth.

Word Watch

advice   advise   royal
courage   proud

The Eagle and the Mole

An eagle flew into a deep forest to find a home for his family. He chose a tall and wide-spreading oak tree as the best place for a nest.

A mole had heard about the eagle's plan to build a nest in the oak tree. He finally gathered enough courage to tell the king of birds, "This oak tree is rotten at the roots and is not a safe place for a home."

The eagle did not accept this advice kindly. He felt that it was not fitting for a mole to advise such a great bird as himself. So he sent the mole away without even a word of thanks.

Then the eagle began the work of building his nest in that wide-spreading oak tree. The proud king soon had the new home ready for the royal bird family.

One windy day the eagle had been hunting for the family's breakfast. He had been away from home for only one hour, but when he returned home he found that the tree had fallen. That wide-spreading oak tree had crushed the mother eagle and the little ones beneath it.

"What a sorry creature I am!" cried the eagle sadly.

From his hole in the ground the mole said, "If you had not been so proud you would have remembered that I live among the roots. I can know for sure if a tree is safe or not."

"I have been punished for my pride," said the eagle. "If I had been willing to take advice from the humble mole, my family would be safe and happy right now."

Stop and Think

1. Who told the eagle that the tree was not a safe place for a nest?

2. How would the mole know?

3. Why didn't the eagle listen to the mole?

4. What price did the eagle pay for his pride?

The Bible Says,

"Pride goeth before destruction, and an haughty spirit before a fall."

Proverbs 16:18

How Kong Fu Got His Name

This is an old story that fathers and mothers in China often tell to their children. It is said that Kong Fu, the little boy in this story, grew up to be one of the great men of China.

Many years ago there lived in China a little boy named Kong Fu. This story will tell you how Kong Fu got his name.

In some parts of China water is very hard to get. It has to be carried from the river in big wooden buckets.

A "waterman" carries two buckets swinging on the two ends of a pole, which he puts across his shoulders.

Many families in China have a great clay jug in the yard. This big clay jug is called a "kong." The waterman pours the water into the kong until he fills the whole kong. He is always careful not to spill any water.

Some families have large kongs which are almost as high as a man. The water in a big kong stays cool even in hot weather.

Kong Fu's father had the finest house and the largest kong in the village. The other children often came to Kong Fu's yard to play around the big clay jug.

One day Kong Fu and three other little boys were playing in the yard. One of the boys, named Soo Ling, climbed up on the kong and began walking around the edge.

"See me walk on the edge!" he cried.

The other boys wanted to show Kong Fu they were as brave as Soo Ling. They climbed up on the kong and walked around the edge.

The kong was so big that they could look down on Kong Fu's head. The water in the kong looked very deep. They felt quite brave to be walking on that high edge.

"Why don't you come up and walk on the edge, Kong Fu," they said. "Are you afraid? Why aren't you brave like us?"

Kong Fu did not want to say he was afraid, but he really was. He was afraid to climb up on the kong and walk on the edge.

Around and around the edge of the kong the boys went. Suddenly Soo Ling slipped and fell with a big splash into the water. Down under the water he went; then his head bobbed up.

"Help! Help!" he shouted.

The other children were so frightened at seeing Soo Ling in the water that they climbed quickly down the side of the big jug. They ran away as fast as they could. Only little Kong Fu was left standing in the yard.

Kong Fu was frightened too, but he did not run away. He thought and thought.

"What can I do to save Soo Ling? I cannot reach him from the edge of the kong. I haven't any rope to throw to him."

Then Kong Fu had an idea. Quickly he ran about the yard until he found a sharp stone. He ran back to the kong and began to pound the clay side with the sharp point of the stone.

Over and over in the same place he hit the kong as hard as he could. The side of the kong was soft, and little bits of clay came off every time he hit it. But it was very thick.

Would he be able to dig through it in time to save Soo Ling?

He could hear Soo Ling still splashing and crying in the water. Pound! pound! pound! he hit the clay kong. At last there was a little hole through the side of the big jug. The water began to pour out in a tiny stream, spilling on the ground.

Pound! pound! pound! a few more times, and the water came pouring out in a big stream.

Very soon there was only a little water left in the kong as Soo Ling could stand up on the bottom. He was soaking wet and crying with fright, but he was alive and safe.

Kong Fu ran out to the field and called his father. His father came, reached in the kong, and pulled out Soo Ling.

"We will not laugh at you again, Kong Fu," said Soo Ling. "You were frightened when I thought I was brave. But when there was real danger, you could do the brave thing."

In China, children are often given their names because of something they have done. After this little boy saved Soo Ling from the kong, he was always called Kong Fu.

Stop and Think

1. Why is the waterman careful not to spill any water as he brings it to the kong?

2. What is the kong made of?

3. Who was really brave? Why?

 Bethlehem   barley   bushel
Naomi   Orpah   Boaz

reapers: people who gather grain at harvest
widow: a woman whose husband has died

Ruth in the Harvest Field

A very long time ago, and in a country very far from this, there lived a woman whose name was Naomi. She was a widow.

She had had two sons. The names of the sons' wives were Orpah and Ruth. But these sons had died.

Then the three women lived by themselves in one family. They were very poor. Sometimes they could hardly get enough bread to eat.

In the country where these women lived, the hot sun sometimes killed the grain. This made life even harder for the three poor women.

Because they were so very, very poor, Naomi thought it best for her two daughters-in-law to go back and each live in her old home.

Orpah did go; but Ruth said she would not leave her mother-in-law alone. She would stay with her as long as they both lived.

After that, there was less food than before. But Naomi had heard that there was plenty of grain in the fields about Bethlehem.

Bethlehem was not far away. So the mother-in-law and this daughter-in-law found their way to that place.

When there, Ruth said to her mother-in-law, "Let me go and get food for you. I will glean after the reapers in some field. I will pick up the stalks of grain that are left."

Her mother-in-law said, "Go, my daughter."

Soon Ruth came to a field owned by a rich man named Boaz. And she began to glean there.

This was in the morning; and Boaz came into the field to learn how the work went on.

Seeing Ruth, he said to the man in charge of the reapers, "What young woman is that?"

The man had heard the story of Ruth and her mother-in-law. He told Boaz about them. Then Boaz spoke to Ruth.

He said, "Stay and glean in this field. Go nowhere else. Whenever you are thirsty, you will find water in the jar. At the noon hour, go and take food with the others. I have heard of your kindness to your poor old mother-in-law."

And he said, "God will reward you."

Ruth went at mealtime and ate with the reapers. They treated her kindly.

Then she gleaned again, till the sun went down. She beat out the grain from the straw; and she had nearly a bushel of barley.

She put the barley into a sack, lifted the sack to her shoulder, and went away to her mother-in-law.

She told her mother-in-law everything that had happened. That night the two women had food enough, and they were glad.

From that time until the end of the harvest, Ruth went, day by day, and gleaned in the same great field.

She and her mother-in-law no longer lacked for food, as they had done in their old home. Now they had plenty.

Long after all the harvest had been gathered, Boaz took Ruth to be his wife. He had seen how kind she had been to her mother-in-law.

Ruth's home was then in the midst of the fields where she had gleaned. Her mother-in-law—who had been so sad—became very happy.

Stop and Think

1. What does it mean to glean in the fields?

2. Why did Ruth work so hard in the fields?

Word Watch

barley　　cushions　　Egypt
Arabia　　Persia　　ancient
　　　　caravans

The Camel

The camel is larger than the horse and is a very strange-looking animal. He is so tall that he is taught to kneel down to have his load put on and taken off and for people who wish to ride to get on his back.

When he rises, he lifts his hind feet first, and a man who is not used to sitting and riding on a camel is very likely to be thrown forward over the animal's head and to be badly hurt by falling on the ground.

One kind of camel has two humps on the back, and another kind has only one. These humps are made mostly of fat. When camels have to go a long time with very little food, the humps become smaller and smaller until they almost disappear.

The camel's stomach is made so that it will hold a large amount of water. He can carry enough water in this way to last four or five days. Sometimes he goes nine or ten days without drinking.

Because of his humps, the camel can live for many days without food. He eats coarse herbs, thorny shrubs, and the leaves and branches of trees. He will also eat beans, dates, and barley cakes when he can get them.

The feet of the camel are large and wide, and on the bottoms of them are thick pads or cushions. These pads are covered with a skin so hard that the hot sands of the desert do not hurt them.

The camel walks with so little noise that you would not hear his footsteps even if he were going along close beside you on rough and rocky ground.

The eyes of the camel are protected from the light and glare of the sun by large, overhanging eyebrows and by very long eyelashes. He can close his nostrils to keep out the fine sand which is raised by a very slight wind in the desert.

The home of the camel is in Africa and Asia. He is of great value to the people in those countries for carrying heavy loads across the wide sandy plains which are found there.

Camels are usually good-natured, gentle, and patient. For thousands of years they have been used in Egypt, Arabia, Persia, and other Eastern countries. In ancient times merchants often traveled in large groups with many camels loaded with goods.

These groups of men and camels are called caravans. Sometimes the camels of a caravan travel one after another in single file. At other times they go side by side, making a line more than a mile long.

Like many other animals, camels are said to be fond of music, and when they become very tired their drivers sing lively, cheering songs.

The caravans are often led and guided by the sound of a bell. When the music of the bell stops, all the camels stop. When the music begins again, they all move forward.

Stop and Think

1. Which is larger, a camel or a horse?

2. Why should a passenger be careful while the camel stands up?

3. How many humps does a camel have?

4. Where does a camel store water for a long journey?

5. How are the camel's eyes protected from the bright sun?

6. What is a large group of men traveling together with camels called?

7. How do camels help people?

Word Watch

violets   autumn

The Seasons

What does it mean when the bluebird comes
And builds its nest, singing sweet and clear?
When violets peep through the blades of grass?—
These are the signs that spring is here.

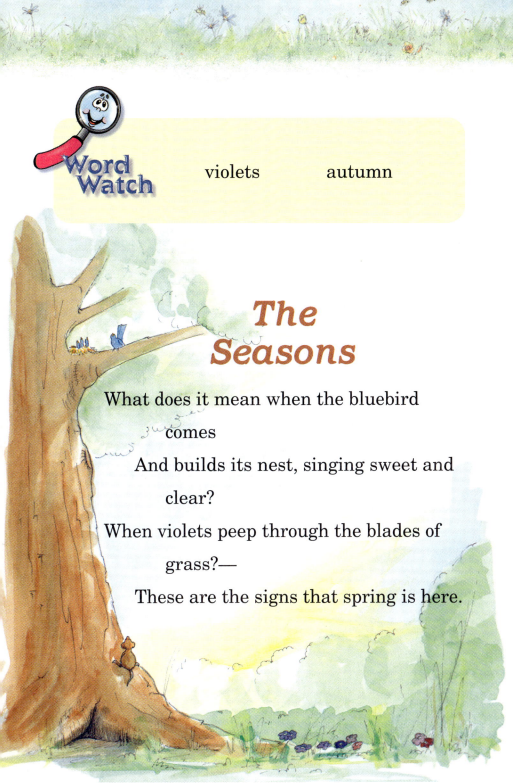

What does it mean when the berries are
>ripe?
When butterflies flit and honeybees
>hum?
When cattle stand under the shady
>trees?—
These are the signs that summer has
>come.

What does it mean when the crickets
>chirp,
And away to the south the robins steer?
When apples are falling and leaves grow
>brown?—
These are the signs that autumn is here.

What does it mean when the days are
   short?
   When leaves are gone and brooks are
      dumb?
When fields are white with drifted snow?—
   These are the signs that winter has
      come.

The old stars set and the new ones rise,
   The skies that were stormy grow bright
      and clear;
And so God's beautiful, wonderful signs
   Go round and round through the changing year.

bonfire   linen
fastened   quiver

The First Balloon

One day two brothers were making a bonfire. Their names were James and Joseph. It was in France about two hundred years ago. The brothers lay on the grass and watched the fire burn.

"What makes the air seem to quiver over the fire?" asked one of the brothers.

"That is the hot air rising," said the older brother. "Hot air is lighter than cold air."

"Yes," said James. "That is what we were reading about the other day. If we fill a paper bag with hot air, it will go up too."

"Wouldn't it be fun to try?" said Joseph. "I can get some of that strong paper which father is making now. We can tie a string around the open end of the bag."

So the brothers made some bags out of the strong paper and held them over the hot coals. The bags went up a little way. Then the air in them grew cold, and they sank down to the ground.

"If we could keep the air hot," said James, "the bags would go up into the clouds."

This was a hard thing to do. The boys thought about it every day.

"If the bag is large and strong, it will hold hot air enough to last a long time," the brothers said.

So they made a linen bag. It was very large. A great crowd of people came to see it go up.

The brothers made a hot fire of straw. The linen bag was held over the fire.

At first it had no shape. Then it swelled out round and full.

"Let go!" cried James. Away went the big bag into the air.

For ten minutes the hot air held it up. Then it came slowly down and was found a mile and a half away.

This was the first balloon. Soon men made balloons which were filled with gas. Gas does not need to be heated, because it is lighter than air. These gas balloons stayed in the air a long time.

After a time, a basket was fastened under the balloon and a man rode in the basket. It was a great sight to see a man ride in a balloon.

Stop and Think

1. What country were James and Joseph from?

2. What made their balloons rise?

3. What was the balloon that stayed in the air for ten minutes made of?

4. What was added to the balloons later so that men could ride in them?

Word Watch

scuttled   mulberry
curious

Angus and the Ducks

Once there was a very young little dog whose name was Angus, because his mother and his father came from Scotland.

Although the rest of Angus was quite small, his head was very large and so were his feet.

Angus was curious about many places and many things:

He was curious about WHAT lived under the sofa and in dark corners and WHO was the little dog in the mirror.

He was curious about Things-Which-Come-Apart and those Things-Which-Don't-Come-Apart; such as SLIPPERS and gentlemen's

SUSPENDERS and things like that.

Angus was also curious about Things-Outdoors, but he could not find out much about them because of a leash.

The leash was fastened at one end to the collar around his neck and at the other end to SOMEBODY ELSE.

But Angus was most curious of all about a NOISE which came from the OTHER SIDE of the large green hedge at the end of the garden.

The noise usually sounded like this: "Quack! Quack! Quackety! Quack!!"

But sometimes it sounded like this: "Quackety! Quackety! Quackety! Quack!!"

One day the door between OUTDOORS and INDOORS was left open by mistake; and out went Angus without the leash or SOMEBODY ELSE.

Down the little path he ran until he came to the large green hedge at the end of the garden.

He tried to go around it but it was much too long. He tried to go over it but it was much too high. So Angus went under the large green hedge and came out on the OTHER SIDE.

There, directly in front of him, were two white DUCKS. They were marching forward, one-foot-up and one-foot-down. "Quack! Quack! Quackety! Quack!!!"

Angus said: WOO-OO-OOF!!!

Away went the DUCKS all of a flutter. "Quackety! Quackety! Quackety! Quackety! Quackety!!!"

Angus followed after.

Soon the DUCKS stopped by a stone watering trough under a mulberry tree.

Angus stopped, too. Each DUCK dipped a yellow bill in the clear cool water. Angus watched. Each DUCK took a long drink of cool clear water. Still Angus watched. Each DUCK took another long drink of cool clear water.

Then Angus said: WOO-OO-OOF!

And the DUCKS scuttled and Angus lapped the cool clear water.

Birds sang in the mulberry tree.

The Sun made patterns through the leaves over the grass.

The DUCKS talked together: "Quack! Quack! Quack!" Then: HISS-S-S-S-S-S-S!!! HISS-S-S-S-S-S-S!!!

The first DUCK nipped Angus's tail! HISS-S-S-S-S-S-S!!! HISS-S-S-S-S-S-S!!!

The second DUCK flapped its wings!

Angus scrambled under the large green hedge, scurried up the little path, scampered into the house and crawled under the sofa. For exactly THREE minutes by the clock, Angus was NOT curious about anything at all.

Stop and Think

1. Which parts of Angus were very large?

2. What things was Angus curious about?

3. Why couldn't Angus find out more about Things-Outdoors?

4. What was Angus most curious about?

5. Did Angus ever find out what the noise was?

| Prussia | stammered |
| honesty | errands |

Frederick and His Page

Frederick the Great, king of Prussia, was a very curious, but also a very clever man. One day he rang the bell for his page to come to him. A page is a little boy who runs errands in great houses, and waits upon people who live there. But when the king rang, no one came to answer the bell.

The king then opened the door, and found the page had gone to sleep. He saw a letter hanging out of his pocket, and, being curious, he took it out and read it. It was a letter from the boy's mother. She thanked him for sending her part of his wages; and said God would reward him, if he continued to serve the king well.

Having read this note, the king went out, got some money, and slipped it into the boy's pockets. Then he went back to his room, and rang so loudly that the page awoke. When he came into the room, the king said, "Surely you have been asleep." The boy stammered out an excuse, and, putting his hands into his pockets, found the money there.

Some boys would have been glad at this, and said nothing about it to any one. But this page was an honest lad, who knew he had not earned the money, and thought it did not belong to him. So he drew it out, pale and trembling, but unable to speak a word.

"What is the matter?" said the king.

"Alas, your majesty," said the boy, falling upon his knees, "some one wishes to do me harm.

I know nothing about this money which was in my pocket."

The king was much pleased with his honesty, and told him to send the money to his mother, as a reward for bringing up her son so well.

We never lose by being honest in everything we do. If this boy had said nothing about the money the king had put in his pocket he would not have been trusted so much afterwards. But when the king had found out how honest he was, he took care to help him as much as he could.

Stop and Think

1. What kind of man was Frederick the Great?

2. What is a page?

3. What did the king learn from reading the letter in the page's pocket?

4. Why wasn't the boy pleased when he found the money?

5. How else did the king reward the page?

The Owl
L. Alma-Tadema

When all the children lie asleep
    And the village lamps are out,
The owl from her lonely nest does creep
    To roam the world about.

Her wings are quiet, her eyes are keen,
    She needs no starry light;
By her each timid thing is seen
    That nibbles in the night.

But when the dawn begins to break
And the morning hour is chill,
She wings her way across the lake,
Or hoots upon the hill.

Now soon the robin sweetly sings,
Unharmed go mouse and mole,
The owl has closed her silent wings,
And sleeps in some dark hole.